Flowers Of Bad

A false translation of Charles Baudelaire's
Les Fleurs Du Mal

David Cameron

Unbelievable 🐊 Alligator

Some of these poems appeared previously in *6 X 6, 6,500, Boog Instant Anthology, The Brooklyn Review Online, canwehaveourballback.com, The East Village, Fence, Lungfull!, Murmur, POeP!, Pom-Pom, Sal Mimeo, Sycamore Review, Transcendental Friend: The Bestiary* & *The World*.

"XXV (You put the universe under your thumb...)" first appeared in *Verses That Hurt: Pleasure and Pain from the POEMFONE Poets* (St. Martin's Press).

Many of these poems were also published in the smaller collections *Flurries of Mail* (Mbira), *Dirty Mom* (Unbelievable Alligator) & *Le Voyage* (Portable Press at Yo-Yo Labs).

The author would like to thank Milton Kessler, Jo Ann Wasserman, Eugene Ostachevsky, Brenda Coultas, Brendan Lorber, Edwin Torres, Kim Lyons, Sharon Mesmer, Paul Dean, Brenda Iijima, Larry Fagin & Katherine McQuarrie for their insights and their support.

The author is also grateful for funding provided by the New York Foundation for the Arts as part of a Fellowship in Poetry which aided in the completion of this project.

Distributed by SPD/Small Press Distribution
1341 Seventh St., Berkeley CA 94710
www.spdbooks.com

This book was published by Unbelievable Alligator in conjunction with Ugly Duckling Presse.

For direct orders please visit www.uglyducklingpresse.org.

www.flowersofbad.com

For Jackson Mac Low,

The Greater Fabricator

TABLE OF CONTENTS

Révolte

La Mort

To The Reader

Dear Reader,
　　These poems are made up of lines. Yesterday
B.I. accused me of not moving deep enough into the engaging part.
What is the engaging part? I wonder honestly
If that's the thing that's been missing all this time.

I think many of these poems are beautiful. I know
That there are people who frown upon the use of
Words like beautiful, but I think the word is still
Quite useful. Too vague? Too elusive or ever-changing

A quality? Probably. But there is still something in
My head which tells me that these poems are
Beautiful. Beautiful and often surprising. I don't
Think B.I. wanted to say that they weren't

Beautiful, just that I wasn't fully taking a risk
In them emotionally, that they were "entertaining"
Perhaps, but not "moving." I'm putting words into her
Mouth, of course. Or at least that I'm not revealing an emotional

Self in my poems. I think that was her complaint.
I have heard some of my contemporaries talking of other
Poets and asking (although the recipients of this question
Are always absent) "Where is your emotional content?" But I've always

Thought my poems *had* emotional content. The
Question hits home though because I know that when I began these
Poems I was trying to get away from ex-
Pressing or trying to represent my emotions in poems.

I felt like I'd done that enough already, and
Wore it out. Now I can't seem how to figure out how
To do what I once did. I can't seem to write "I"
In a poem which doesn't somehow transform me

Or at least offer the option of transforming
The speaker or supposing that he/she is someone other
Than me. I think that it might be more accurate to
Say that the emotional content of these poems

Comes through, but indirectly. At least four of these are

Love poems, and there are a few other dedications.
Did I really slap my friend Gabe red in the face singing?
Well, maybe at some point, but "like a butcher?" Not that I

Can recall, but the emotional joy I feel towards him comes
Through. And many of the emotional responses that I have to these
Poems came about long after I wrote them. What emotional
Content of yours is in these poems? How do they resemble you?

To The Reader

Sorry, but cataract my eyes being flummoxed   *busted*
Sorry, how can I avoid being influenced by the copy of this I read before
oceanliner
    the fisherman pulling in his line
fiancé opens ...with a club, the three and bawling over or bowl-
Or occupying all of France again with a forthright bouquet? Our spirits
ing over warthogs the masses haven't worsted wool and trombones , assets
    have worked or our noses have worked and travelled and our
bodice dustbin
    bodies, dead in the kitchen
moose   fish   gallant aces
Eating, hanging from a noose or finally getting over a cold. Do you like
recipe   over   rhinoceros
    record stores do you sneeze
carumba astin martin pernod a whalebone corset
When your typewriter puts up a comma and not a period or when the
on the lawn
    nurse feeds you porridge because your own arms are immobile you're
kelvin   rabbits add up
    immobilized by tetanus, rabies and you're waiting for the vaccine.

shoreline   seagulls.
Our fishermen or sharp-tongued songbirds or our house painters back
    again to paint over painted walls, They paint over the locks
fixture, the light
So every effort we make to fit the key in We hang up the noose on the
frustrated, the president rolls over on his side
    sprinkler pipe but it's freshly painted and we have to go to the
treasure island in the east pray old view
    hardware store and pay for our new rope with greasy hands.
    Haven't we met?
And we were both walking in the same door in a general sense we both
house of zen pastry underdark
    attended the ball in honor of the factory and drank bourbon with
shouting
    the chemist
I never thought Helen of Troy an ape-man would cry for a devil-man or
    bathe our paperclips.

Over, wasn't it, the ear-horn of evil or isn't it Satan in his third
brimmaster, a coffee-maker
    trimester
newspaper on
Who pays for our drinks with whale bone, a long tongue our notepaper in
the present, or alimony his
    pastels already half sung.
art the train   gopher,   too?
Do we eat the thin gold foil too? Do we vote? are we voters and each picks
    a letter out
mississippi gone or my the atheist
All is steaming and parsed, split and the chemist knew

how many times   tried
How to say all the new fancy double-talk that tied the ropes up the many
remotely a camera
    fingers we remember on the cash register
squid   torn
All the little squished things we've turned over the earth we've turned over
over time, make payments
    the small grapes and meals
That each day sing to us from the wood-stove. Each day we go down the
    teeth of a mastodon stomping loudly
Bravely towel   *and two*
But you're not afraid. The sandman O the beach the green wheat my arms
sugar shakers,   always allowing canaries in.
    celebrate who can spit between their teeth.

doesn't caring . so forth for frost out of the   garden.   the holy post box.
Aint she dainty crowning setting foot out of the bathtub and her poor skin
torrid under the tooth autumn turner. Where, Cold old coat
    tells the truth or the turkey was good to eat

Issue #7. Around the house she causes cousins railroad crossing

It had a wound. It had seen the virgin mother coming up out of an
   antique litter box
wings   osteoporosis
And we wanted to see it grow old in a monastery with swings out back
Then toasted praise be. Towels. Tonsils. The towel rack.
Then we pressed too hard on the comma key and along came They
shoshone. Powergrid or toothache in any pantry.
   unveiled the pulled back the orange curtain

And angels were going to cut my hair tonight. Or
And angels had burned it. Four million on the march to comment briefly
motion   monitor Constantly.
   on a million or controlling the boat in the
and the cannon resorts
Danube. I feed the cows rubberized Somebody Nobody from a family
   of demons
toweled off. depression
And when we breathe, lumbering into the mustard closet
Down into it, into snow or soft or not seen with sourdough instead of shoes

If the violin leaps up onto us or leaps onto the yardstick our lawn catching fire
Aunt Nonie's serious storm clouds brown or grey   or grey   antidote
And Aunt Nonie moves her hurt from here to you and her brocading and
coma acres   to we reach
   the cards come across the table smoothly as adultery or false gods
plantain,   someone hold me
Sneakers plain sneakers subtly underscore where the animals fall into the
are you the dentist?
   earth Our intention for tuna
Is discovered by a friend. "¡Mira!" booms over the moors but it's not
   Thomas Hardy's accountant.

Persimmons one nile fever toting a yardstick   forest   shall clutch or cherish the Little
Permit me, if you will, to mention these few small charcoals of the Little
Richard
   Rascals gang each posed mounted on the back of a lice-ridden panther,
With burned fingertips and no eyebrows, with a corporation dedicated to
june bug versus hurricane
   lifting their trousers well over the towers. Unless snakes
Or a lemon-tree monster claps his hands and throws a sheepskin full of egg nog
allow me to introduce
Into the manager's house of famous german nose-vices
Mercury is somewhere in here
There will always be more people who are sledding, more people packed
now
   into the machinist's office, more times that I am maudlin
And coughing up the seagull feathers you've pushed effortlessly into my silent
Garth Brooks   a shallow wading pool
Furnace. Who's cokeing iron pigs with free labor? Who's small potatoes are
not just another or any old boxing match
   grown in a trash heap?
can you play guitar, sailor?
Irishmen in the battlements have and level their lemondine avalanche.

and then he married my high school   sweetheart
So I guess this is the end for us. We're splitting up. The oil the battery is
   full but leaking involuntarily.
should I be in tears?
She dreams of already warm hunting dogs smoking in the hookah.
I hide in a closet
You know all this stuff already, reader, sea monster in the delicatessen
this means you   gila monster
—Needle-phobic reader—my seeming mirror babbler—monster with a lisp
   and a fluffernutter sandwich.

4

SPLEEN ET IDÉAL

I
Benediction

Before I loan out my every secrets to the captain of the singers
The poet, a ghost in this world annoys
The same year the hairdresser's ghost, and she is as plain as a train in a
      tunnel passing.
The crisp air, ping-pong on the lawn And do you? Who takes my place on
      the cake

And ah, haven't I missed at least the bottom of the sea? A rolling. A Norseman
The planets' hats and our laughter, small women. Her dress is smaller
Speaking in the night rain and on a plane the captain undresses the shoeless
Where my concubine wears my windbreaker my death. The revocation of
      my library card.

You take my wallet having chosen to enter the woman. All the women
Pouring out the canoe of never three, or sad, or the queen.
And then I seem not from off stage but a daring financier
With a wad of bills and valentines a dog ate its way through my living
      room. Boat captain

I am a wolf. Having been to jail twice your hair who opens the door, at least.
On the instrument swimming After all, the childhood tree-chopper
And I turn to you well & sit the tree of the miserable purse-snatchers
A pen won't hang upside down the buttons on her blouse undone. The
      approaching storm

She shows me the cloud cover, the poor excuse with no napkin
And, don't misunderstand me, she's a hussy. A shy, egg-timing hussy in nylons
She writes the letter around. From the great hen's nest
Consecrated by butchers my mother stole her lunch.

Above all, beneath the gossiping the basement, a lunch.
The child is given a bottle of wine goat cheese and sun
And in all things, this pen it and all the cows or the stewards
You find me again among the desserts and the green nectar.

He plays with the wind can he use the soup spoon in the mirror
And soon the truth in the song shut-ins already having had their lunch
And the water in the air on your suit a bird. A fishing bird. An ancient
    fisher-bird
Are you crying because you see the body shop remember the birds in the trees?

All those that the wind wants to love hardly one tower worth crushing
    with a wrecking ball
Or as well the hard lads spitting a train full of owls
The churchmen breaking into broken Fords & Toyotas she, he pulls on the
    plants at tea
And those who find the documents on his person and what are we to make
    of the moon's ferocity

In the loaf of bread and my insides fall out of your mouth.
They battle for cinders in the street and a necktie stolen at the funeral.
With a blood shortage they throw starts at a touch
And do you smell an army of miserly she their steps & the Easter Bunny?

Your wife is going to crinkle public places.
"He's a thief and I've found what of it? She's mine, I love her
I'm making a meter maid out of idle hands pineapple hosiery in the cupboard.
And with them I would like to find myself she makes me drive cars again

And I'm sorry, my trousers fell in the mud up North buttermilk, from the
    census bureau a shuffle
After new muscle-machines in the jungle mountains and a goddess of feet
Who can say if I'm a thief the lump sum under the door
Or if your soup is in your laughter. These men whizzy wizards of feet!

And when I'm adding numbers even these the forests
I stand with a bad attitude. My frail that, and a the water main
And the angles, parallel lines what lines it up, the nudes, the pubic mound
Or didn't you say that until the sunken galleon in the hallway the factory a
    battle amongst cooks

Just like a young bird then and if the water the lock shaking and the
    doorknob rattling
I reach for a spider. The curtain at tea the red season
And, if only to raise again the subject of my bad habits you are my favorite.
I throw him from the terrace. and with you the great whale.

Towards the ceiling, where the sonnets are I seize this. I see a sort of holy
    subway ride combing the library
The poet would say herein lives my eyelashes arms apart

And the call of the west a fish tank
She undresses, and at last from the riot, the mob.

"Do you drink soy milk? Do you crouch and throw dice or was it you who
        gave me such a plane ticket
Like a divine cardiologist to the smelling station
And like the best on the avenue the gas pump. The most of them
Who builds the treehouses once saints for dinner.

I know that you're protecting On the street I met a poet.
In the clock tower kiss the days before saints rode lion-back
And that you've invited yourself later or never. The party.
From old trains, from the real Tuesday for days accepting cans of soup.

I know that sleeping in the east Saint sewing machine
Where more will never run out of closet space the terrace, I eat fire for her
And if it's my fault that your hair falls out or should I? What do you sing?
        Crown Heights stays with me but no flowers yet
I suppose that all the temperatures in all my empty vases.

But the young girls forget and the antique friendly fire tree.
The metals never knew it's pearls that might be iron
You vote for a hand climbing your thigh you can't always start the engine
The lady draws a beautiful card from between them and easily from your chair

Because it's already a done deal and the light is a mouthful of light
You wait in the doorway to rob the saint it's thin rays of ifs or ironing
And aren't these your dead eyes it is. It's in the spoken-for advance of her
        car's tires
Sing now, some mirrors only fogged up and clearly shiftless!

II
The Albatross

Solve this: for amusement my favorite detective carries home
A pregnant albatross under his sea-blue vest.
Who should follow but that lazy bunch from his sea voyage.
They come gliding along on ice skates, then one trips and bloodies his
       gums on the concrete.

The pain some have even though they're not sick bends me to the surfer's
       point of view
That rows of chess players on the boardwalk malign the sea, haunt it
lazily. 'Tis a damn pity, the grand leers they make at the white squares
As though they made up the front of an ice truck. Training on the coast

This traveler lost his gloves, his title, and for what?
Lay on your back in a row boat, get laid, read a comic.
An ape's belly could break your heart with its brutish, gauloise
Laughter. A botanist is the same. He foliates on his infirmities.

What does a poet look like? is he the prince of nudes?
These questions haunted me when the musicians were rioting for Joan of Arc.
In the end, at least the sour sun tastes the best of my hues
And sails them out giant-sized, as fish in a marching band.

III
Ember

Below the embers, below the ventilators,
Medications, backgrounds, naiads, medications,
Beyond the salamander, beyond the embers,
Beyond the checkrooms of existential salamanders,

My ember, you mirror with accomplishment,
And, like a beetle-browed naiad who paints in the oracle,
You grammatically select the pastoral ibis
With an imperial and Maltese ventilator.

You erupt lynx-eyed from these Maltese medications;
Veer to paint yourself in the seventh accomplishment,
And bark, like a pastoral and dinerous laboratory,
The converted fellow who revolts the lean embers.

Behind the embers and the vadose checkrooms
Who characterize from lynx-eyed pentagons beetle-browed embers,
Hard-pressed checkrooms painting from a vadose accomplishment
To erupt towards the seventh lean checkroom!

Checkrooms dissolve the pentagons, like accomplishments,
Towards the checkrooms the medication paints an existential laboratory.
—Which paints on the ventilator, and characterizes without embers
The laboratory of flowers and of Maltese checkrooms.

IV
Correspondances

Nature sing out on our broken sunglasses. Lean alive
In the cold slow mailroom misdirecting our sentences.
Pass by my apartment on your way to the forest of symbols
With money in your pocket, looking forward to those familiar faces.

When you resound in the hallway stand proud being vegetarian,
So the dog wouldn't bite your arm on the beach, but joined your side, spitting.
The pause between this room where you sleep and the wine singing in
      your head
Leaves the smell of cold days you've borrowed, and the tropical ones now
      returning, looking for payback.

Your kind has its hands meddling deep in baby carriages, searching an
      office in a frenzy,
Taking the lead in a sad dance. Hotheads may try to do you in with a smile
      and a lead pipe against your forearm
But only an actress' body & beautiful wealth will win you over.

Are you sure that thieves houses aren't too full with uncatalogued booty?
The stars burn red-brown with hot music released by brave scientists.
Quit carrying on from the wheelchair of your spirit and lay the cold water
      out on a new morning of the senses!

V
Blanche

Je suis esporié quand il vient en près du casson cassé

Et tu oublis à lamonir tes garoles. Il roule descendement l'escalier de la
maison de garné—un trou-rouleur.

Et quoi si diloncie ou les archers Romains et la femme menne à la dejeuner?

Vient ça, et moi ma chanson est comme bonne comme et avec emonité.

Et le ciel et qui est en amour avec les maurins geffluant dans le pûle au-mélu?

Au-souf l'escalier et à la toilette. Maintenant regardons à la chassile. Je suis
garrant, tu es Chinoise.

Le cygne est souffé. Quiles des mooles—

Je ne voit pas le point de cette parlisson et un garçon soi-plein ou plonte
ses dints et combien? Seulement

En Mai aimons-nous un baigniette de pain à cette mode. Une oule volait
mon cigar. Il cloussait vigement et puis au-souf et en toné au-coule
toute blanche nos robes à des corde des garments.

Avril dit l'univers et ses tintinabulations sont abbrivé sûr les gines

Et si diloncie ou s'elle ne l'arrive jusque, elle est aronsé par un ordinateur.
Après tout, qui a le droit

Être un aviateur et quelque journées j'aronse au-souf contre les nominées
pour la chaliste de la brigage de l'aschifferie.

Fruité par pûr ou si par l'orange sûr la verge d'un gyre à l'Alzheimers.

Et n'était-il pas la chaise ou de moins une ferme soit donnait des goûts
des pommes!

Poudrères aujourd'hui, quand ils veulent vous batter sûr la tête avec un
piano de concert

Ces journaises nationale ou bureaux de postes et l'ensconce des pieds dans
le fleuve. Un soule de fides

Le gournoncé des hommes et aussi des femmes

N'est-il pas prêt de la pour nous une petite village des ponce-de-ouf et
bureaux de postes et n'êtes-vous pas quelqu'une fameuse

Devant moi maintenant dans ce nuit et mostilant au-déla à une chambre
des prêves un cocilateur pour un gorçeau?

O mes étoiles et les dentorontés de mon officier de truance multiplicant et
dans les modes de l'année passé!

O toniques de gaz soufflant! touristes qui neglegerent pas les mosques!

O pauvres hommes de soulangéres tombant au-déla somantés dans les cassins et
chauvrement gossant-de-tête ou en dulant vos nouveaux thermeuses

Un cadeaux des dieux des utilités, pertolousé, et vous mensez les deaux de
vos mains

Et vous le pedrez à vos pieds. Vous e-postez Martina Navritilova dans sa
aeroplane boutré!

Et vous, femmes satrés, quoi l'enfer est—?

Au-déla mon chalfeu ou en risant mes giardinées. Un jeun garçon avec un
 pronce à son pied et vous, guy-thé-vert,
Vous m'osez une victoire ou vichysoise. Une petite voiture un train et
 j'apprendais tout à les eux à dix.
Et tout ces drône-voleurs en maquisent derrière la glaze de la douche
 attendent à vonté du merde sûr moi.

Nous avons un très mais à la gauche vous allez voir la terre de jeux des
 josses de lions.
O gens! N'êtrez pas et je pense de ces en vous à bateaux en jaurissant les
 véloumens pour le BIF
Mais qui dit que quand nous laisson la fenêtre ouvert nos muses entrent en
 visage-noir.
Neptune et toujours il aimait une endive tant quelqu'un à sa salade.
Il me dessinait une portraite d'une jeune fille à buste massé mais fameuse
 en bêne.
À cette fille sainteurante voncé aux mûrs à la face de mon édifice plongant
 une dorge lequel a était silente depuis avant je parratonais,
À la loyaliste rianquant dans le chûne et clair contre ou seulement une
 bustine d'eau
Et qui va à reparranter mon apartement avec bamboo? Sûr sous en les
 scientistes maurais du Jamaican stud poker
Comme les ciel-monçeurs, ces ou n'est pas toutes et les fleurs
Ses parfums, elle et une fois je tombais à dans une facile, souffle lit-de-
 grosses, mais c'était à elle!

VI
Hep Slears

Reubens, dile sijo fanbev, are praed su dell su,
On erraid lue meith chule or aran prole ceif ei,
Fast miule ae cavesse fei til soanes gassue,
Alt clam rel sen clam oi ran alm mares de die;

Léonard de Vinci, emti pindrooms or fobrer,
Nou des anx varmex, car goots sauce duusni
August eees dat mobstry, taaline caper phom rer
Prines gepeti squeels as dirm dae cults ferny;

Rembrandt, rostrume lopit traut it merm phile deus,
And grenidor teen ef ex tucce cuild murs,
Alirae en phlurs delpee sourdere xsoures,
Et durnn veretab quaer dohvey mit snerurs;

Michel-Ange, vuud elgaus noe loit oive Hercules
Vo mer ets do-rel Christs, ee stad risee tseltu
Squadi ness slup taf scenome pra des stine scules
Hriedaile donurg lein treast reins retuce tu;

Sudinose peemel, fruxec brouce dadnee,
Ouquli art rabides ma saute es ses goujats,
Dourd belglerc grognaile maum une fothe de joenie
Puget, comequiel nes lurpeace fer dormats;

Watteau, use salient launer vere coidocils scrub,
Praidem seemst frone colb, penny noi talmal,
Deiar fess treissal des regolare clerc setrup,
Qui lefty trains an ocean oover bleutal;

Goya, coalspace much eerns deincon shineu,
Aerleude aub dost fumes if consuite iquabi ast,
Suitelles rane tomise vourn danf teteid sue,
Strenton aud enu tlersjaem urb ep sibol nast;

Delacroix, gatels ahd vinn maecau ges ad saens,
Aujomerv ori bade sisgon upt burpos stare,
Nurf, laefeth god-can eis, raugoine us sersans
Pif, poon ecundase mote tumsuse fer Weber;

Seems bilincotap, seems calphide, seens clacts,
Eats gulir, sems dex, seers cesc, seps ce cettu,

Ram blup ohlehter onir ait dinleen sacts;
Nessel pum lin cimture sud vouscri oper too!

Repesteenl crustae per climel linets ni
Yonder xipoom lurpoe veer liver tran,
Tusha smerp allumnae culs dille gritelee
Dapeln scurso pedsi shad sens spues rule baud gran!

Ragee-tragee, Seigneur, lonct eivmim sarm lunt leice
Sen so qreger ein dots ne dounti dispounun
Doe tanqagog lauqlur nuce tet deene ar geis
Vi bur teo dridit merto tura treevee none!

The Sickened Muse

My poor muse, alas! what have you done this morning?
Your crossed eyes are populous with dreamy visions
And I see from tower to tower reflections on your tainting
Of folly and horror, cold and stuffed.

The green succubus and the pink lunchtime,
Have they crossed the poverty and the love of your urinals?
The coachman, from a despotic and mutton-chopped pogo-stick,
Has he gnawed at the foot of the fabulous mint factory?

I would breathe the smell of the sanitization
Your walk-through vision must always visit,
And the blood in your calibrated underwear from a musical parade

Like the numbered sounds from old words
Which ring out from tower to tower as the father of songs,
The bus driver, the big pan, the oldest of moustaches.

The Venerated Muse

O muse of my dog, amounting to pails,
Will you, when January latches onto its bored,
Sneeze nights out around us from snowy evenings,
A boxer to drive us with two purple feet?

Will you rain down stolen marbles
On waxy dreams that fish for our wallets?
Will you send your kiss to Autumn's momentary palace
And recount the gold of voter's assurances?

It is necessary to earn your daily bread
Like the child of a washerwoman, to play with fire
And sing *Te Deum* with jewels clutched in your jaw

Or stand on the riverbank and join stars to your coat tails
And your laugh will trample the rain with blindness,
The poor taking their money from the opening of your vulgar mouth!

IX
The Lemonade Man

The sun shines on an oil slick at the bottom of the reservoir
But a new wind is rolling slowly in from Rome.
Don't lift it, don't turn your nose up in bigotry. Try
To laugh as ten Parisian men would at the sight of one of their
        countryman milking a cow.

This shampoo may stop dandruff, but when your boot
Comes off in a mudslide you'll wish you'd never disparaged
The winds of Italy, and pray for their return. For one Italian hurricane
You'll sacrifice lambs, or fast, or curse your friends with hemorrhoids.

When I met him, he was girlish, but now he's older and a pacifist.
The Pope slinks around in the deep Chinatown night, but that's par for
        the course. At his age, it's not unusual
To want to tie-up any number of sticky murders. *"How many have I drowned?!*

Will they ever stop haunting me? Will I ever be free of
The ghosts of Chinatown and cowering like a dog in a corner while two thieves
        fish under my mattress for the garrote that strangled Miss America?
The police file on me stands as high as eight short men! I murdered the mayor!"

X
To A Loan Shark

I never know what fruits these arms will bear.
My feet carry me singing through the brightly lit streets
And sometimes safes fall on my head, sometimes the rain. Once the phone rang
Like a bird singing in a garden where all the fruit had been eaten.

There are things I have felt under the hood of an auto
That will make use of buttons and rationale
To put the flooded earth back together again by nine o'clock
Before the water creeps up between my toes

And who knows if the new aeroplanes I'm dreaming up
Will find themselves shot cleanly into the sun
Or a mysterious malfunction will empty their fuel tanks?

O bank men! O unemployment checks! Time gobbles up my life
And the shifty-eyed loan shark drunk at the end of the bar
Puts an interested quarter in the juke box and leans over to whisper his
         rank lies into my ear.

May (The guy gone)

Pouring the liquid on the feet of the Lord,
Sisyphus, he had a lot of coinage!
He'd been eaten by dogs older than him.
"Thou art long and time is short," he said.

His loins were like a famous sculpture
Carried off from an island of the dead.
He called my name and paused to shake his violin
Then smacked away the calendar into the fireplace.

May joyously darted up my sleeve
And danced ten fingers as a breeze over my wheat.
He fucked me well near the pinochle table on the beach;

May bloomed out from under my cuff with regret.
Now his soft perfume like a young boy's secret
Dances throughout my thick studies of the sunset.

XII
This Anti-Terror Life: III

Only but ever before the doorway and still. Openish, but soothingly
Not the cathedral, the bells. Somehow you spot the sun on, your snake is
        irresistible or twenty fires and firetrucks
But there you are. The fireplace has a mantle understandably
But between you and me, this evening in the swamp, the harpies and the
        basilisks—hoo boy!

Only us, for hours and the plane rolls 180° in its sleep. Where are you
        this afternoon
Aunt Helen opens up a pastry store a candy store a jewelry store doesn't
        she or at least selling watches and jam
Or and could you be quietly jelly in the prison yard? Cat burglars skulking
        not slinking, osteo-
Porotic and somehow in all this mess you find a place to sit and I'm staring
        at you.

How could you or don't you don't you ever want to sneeze in the woods?
        like olden days and farmers pausing during hurricanes
Or the barn door won't stay shut. The terrace of blue cutting across the
        voice of the speaker, his trousers
Also aflame. Your neck in the cave, also aflame now and how many birds how

And every now and then a nun. I like flowers, your trousers
& isn't it what you've worked for all these years, the blooms in two
        surrounding the fire house
Or out of the faucet. O don't tell me to relax I don't I don't chime in with
        church bells.

XIII
Bohemians Take A Trip

That prophetic tribe of tree pruners
Made its way over here yesterday on their little way
To the Spanish second, where books fire their appetites
On the window sill, ready to be compared with animal feet.

Men throw sour leers at the moon's feet
Along the road to Rome. They've blotted out
All recollection of our walk to the restaurant in the sky.
By the morning they had left, and my best china too.

How fond I've grown of yellow sea birds.
Watching them fly by I nearly drove off the road.
The constellation they've learned to love is green as a pasture.

Don't make ice for the flowers of the desert,
Before this trip you'd forgotten all about liquids.
Empiricism is familiar again, but what holds the future?

XIV
Man & The Sea

In books you're always looking at the sea!
The sea is your mirror, you look like an ass
In the infinite derailments on your street
And your spirit is less patriotic than a golf ball.

You want to jump onto the scene with your image,
But you're embarrassed by your eyes and your arms, and your heart
Was so distracted several times by rumours
Dropped onto your plate that it made your hair unmanageable, indomitable,
       savage and brown.

You are always both a violin player and discrete.
Pal o' mine, the empty set sounds like it's in love with your engineering.
O sea, the empty set knows what's in your security deposit box
And the aunt who's buried her secrets in your backyard.

And because the violin is a very cold instrument
That you battle without pity or remorse,
Like a bank teller you love blood and death.
O round-the-clock looters! O trophyless brothers!

XV
Don Juan In Furs
(what the fuck is mugissement?)

What did Don Juan want with a hot tub careening into the Western Wind
      like a borrowed car?
Had everything that could have been done *been done?* Had the final
      oarsman been made to make music with a butter churn?
Had our calendars been marked for when Leo would burn bright red
      among the constellations like a smattering of antihistamines
Or had he only been told that the only cure for the gonorrhea he'd
      acquired from the airline stewardess was to wear her thin wooden
      bra and to swing his arms about maliciously at any flying thing?

As he climbed the stairs he could feel everybody looking at him, and he
      began to wonder whether this was because he was wearing so
      many large gold medallions and thought that perhaps his lemur-fur
      coat had been unreasonably priced.
Drunken women kept twisting his feet towards the North Star
And sleeping there, knocked out completely unconscious, were a group of
      virgins who'd been ripped off buying tickets for a circus where the
      audience was offered the chance to put their heads into the lion's
      mouth/whose tent collapsed on them once they'd entered/that
      didn't exist.
At last he found the lug nut that had disappeared following a long series of
      muggings, singing with the hoboes in a cattle car.

He laughed to himself looking over the speech his lug nut had prepared
      for him. The Ganges
Was slowly winding down Loisaida Avenue, and like a giant donut
A tax collector in a stolen tow truck came tumbling out of the mountains
      to foreclose
On his own wooden leg. He made some joke about how *A Streetcar
      Named Desire* was written about him,

And suddenly it got a lot colder. The patron saint of the U.S. Post Office
      whose spangled white leather gloves made her look like a cheap
      Elvis impersonator
Lumbered over to read to the members of the British press assembled
      there, more out of love than admiration, a note she'd tucked into
      her breast pocket.
It looked as though the lug nut was sitting with a very large pout on its face,
And our hero threw a bucket of water on it and on the Prime Minister.

All droll Danes should stay in their closets along with their grandfathers
      and rock collections
And this law should be posted and repeated and recopied and displayed in
      every parking lot.
I'm sorry that I've gotten so far off the track of our heroes, who certainly
      have been patient, cutting up lemons for our drinks with their rapiers,
Watching the farmers collect their wheat and not saying a word since
      last Christmas.

Chatiment De L'Orgueil

Chess is the temporary revolution of God's marvelous hour,
Brushing teeth at night time, saving the enraged.
One remembers that one day one of the biggest doctors
Avoided the strong leaves, killing anyone left in his will indifferently.
Was he less afire than France today? less aflame than green-burning stars?
Each chemist screams out articles alone but is unknown.
Each hour they push their zealous spirits into beta-ray Venuses
Like a home to ancient veterans too high on flowers
To worship society's newest train. With the devil's eye
They cry for Jesus, grabbing their little asses, pushing them into the air!
Their nurses and attendants know it's useless,
Their minds are guarded as much as those green stars,
And through a series of knee jabs, reduce them to babies again.

Immediately we ask reason of our god.
We climb the soft stairs alone towards discovery.
All the chaos that rules in the city of intelligence
Is a temple sustained otherwise by torture and opulence.
Beneath its floors is tucked the pavilion of greater fanfare.
The silence in between holds together the din,
As in a cafe where the mouth produces
The legends that are later spoken on the street.
The queen goes to sands to ripen her sight, on the way
Those not her equals separate the grains, digging themselves in to hide.
Sold, finished, and laid out as one would wish,
She brings, at last, her joy and the sunrise.

Beauty

I am a bell o mortals! like a rocky river,
And my favorite scene is where each fish is murdered from vacation spot to
      vacation spot
And their miserable fates inspire a love poem.
I turn the train around thus, and quietly sip champagne with my mother.

Hear me drone on blue, blink staring at the true north.
I unite a heart of snow and the whitener of swans;
I'm as hip as the movement replacing these lines.
I never cry jam. Never onto my crackers.

These poets, they want my big inclinations
Cos I've got the trunk of an elephant in my house, and other fearful
      monuments.
Leisurely, I buy up everything, even the antlers right off the deer studying
      my headlights.

The car I own pours fascination into these docile animals,
Purrs silver and spells all things amounting to bells:
My eyes, my large eyes look back into their clarity, forever.

XVIII
Date Of Stradivari's Death

These were never those in jam jars or these in butterflies over small fishing
        ships sitting on girls' long hair strands
All for a night or a dull thud on third avenue. A bird's nest finished me a
        reptile a dinosaur grabbed me by my shirt sleeve roughly and led
        the way
These feets were broken during the renaissance these fingers washed ashore
        or caught in the nets
A lizard was satisfied the toll plaza and one shallow dog came to show me
        his bone.

I laugh at Garrett's knees, stroke her free of bathwater, red
Or her she trips over the threshold the doorway a little and sneezes. She
        begins her tea on one foot and all
Because I am unable to find the slip cover permit me these my whitened
        arguments
Or one doesn't fly over with keys in hand and re-assemble the water table
        towards my red ideal.

All the feathers fall out the bar is closest to my heart a detective brings us
        to the landfill.
Isn't it you, the demystifier, the wing commander touching asleep with
        fingers wrapped around the edges of the curtain? You raise the
        price of a good lay in your cream
My engine burns out and I crawl along shuddering, cold or climbing an
        old tree for days at a time in Autumn.

O good you, worker bee, grenadier of nights fitted with angels' boots
Twisting away over cigarette butts. We pass quietly through wheat fields.
        We wait for the train to pass through our flower bed.
Ten or so of our detractors rise back up from the lunch table unable to cut
        our kisses down with mountains!

XIX
The Giant

Sometimes Nature in her quick wit
Conceives of the young monsters
I used to love. We lived next door to the house of a giant
With feet as large as a river, and a flowing vocabulary.

I used to love to see her lay down on her side in a snow bank
And storm about freely in her terrible games.
Do you think her heart held a somber flame
To heat the steam swimming behind her eyes?

How can I explain that she looked like Lois Lane?
Shall I run through the list of her enormous generosities?
Sometimes in Summer, when the sun blew open like a sailfish,

This girl would follow a stream from its font all day across the countryside
And fall asleep nonchalantly against a brown hill
Like a quiet hamlet at the foot of a mountain.

The Young Girls

The very horses were nude and put my heart in a jar.
She wasn't watching the sea because of her young girls screaming.
Don't the rich dress him in hand-me downs? The air conditioner
Questions their days, the hours they squirrel away, and their morals.

When he threw in Dan's lap his hot comb and make up kit
The world was in ribbons of metal and sea breeze.
I was hungry for old coffee, though I love the fury
Of choices where school marms battle the light.

She gave the mother of her country a lovely couch to lay on
And above the divan she put lemons at their ease.
The sun loved to lean softly on her like the sea,
Singing her a mountain top from out its valise.

Their eyes fix me like a tiger in a junk shop,
Smoke having blown dreamily as she sat down to draw the flowers.
Hot wax poured slick across her finger
Giving a soft charm to her changes.

Her bra and her jaw, her spoon and her lassoo,
Smooth secret agents hurry by with a swan.
Clairvoyants in police cars passing before my vision
And her wind and her sails like grapes on the vine.

She goes forward, more calmly than a bad painter
To trouble the garbagemen that my donkey has been misplaced,
That the exterminator's handgun has traveled.
Able to deal with it all she sits on her ass and sucks licorice.

I went east to see her in a new dress,
The legs of the antelope broke through while we were drinking.
Her aunt's long story made us resort to the basin
Where certainly the wild water was brown and quite stinging.

—And the lamp was resigned to mourn,
So the soul of the hallway illuminated the bedroom.
Each time she eats a flamboyant dinner
She fills this song with a little more amber!

A.M. Sequel

A saturnine quest ate language. I re-closed all odes.
To Christine S., hurt pear at ease.

Gents, consider mole-free planets or concerts
Exposed to cumulus clouds. Can Iran lend
Iceland eleven sugar beets or send a ton of lice
To murmur ever in Mecca? I excel, am mute. Fate,
Can a neutron bomb end time? I'm lit, deserve
To see us put out in X-rated films. Report ruses,
Recapture hundreds of lions in minutes. Police R

Trains. Six of us pursue I.O.U.'s. I've cut love
Out of a Tennessee ox's tail, am pure
As Clorox queens outing a lemon guru or deer urg-
Ing rugged Artemis' dazed Actaeon. Eve, C-
Notes continue thru "Caravan," quit—a dud. I
Leapt over our ocean. A lone plum met me. Pull
Out aces Ted and jeer at me. Ted tee-
Ters. Steve McQueen and I long to exile all chains
Or dust the Pope's Saab on Route Ten. Can our au-

To liberate super speed for Allah's a.m.
Broadcast, "Live From the Pit?" Anon, pure mule-men
Shall eat a pine cone. In September, ether, rum

Nurses and numb con men quiet our squares on cue.
I am quavering geese. I use Excel. D.C. I care,
And over time I rip Greece's coat. Crete
Can't believe it all, etcetera. As free
As Aquaman—even freer—I billed Crete
A five lepta fee. A mugger quivered. A blue nun
Pursued our uncle to Mexico on a bus. Ted is
Ever beaming Mao's men on Mount Everest en-
Tire loads of Texas' deluxe luau-fruit jelly. A qui-

Et eel people e-mail quiet polar bears e-luau fruit.
I'm never quiet at a luau and hiss, pestering mice,
Oxen, quail and moles, gents. The furry camel left.

I never sleep. Queens leap. A cruel luce el-
Evated requiems. Pele crept. Lice quell a lo-
Quacious quilter. G-Men fax our future. I just ax
A requiem into shards, dunce-face. All I've ever
Considered Ma, are emus I just met up on a moon.

XXI
Song Of The Boat Shoes

Have you come from the profound heavens or do you sort your laundry in
    the Wascomat?
O Beauty, the heavy look wrapped in whaleskin on my dining room table
Confuses these poems with ice cream sellers and crime stoppers
And they both won't leave my wine cellar until I compare you to Pennsylvania.

In your zits a continent of halos has sat down.
You snap rubber bands up through smoke stacks like an orangutang of
    the evening.
Your kisses are a filtre and your mouth is an armoire
That writes the names of heroes on the sides of milk trucks with the hands
    of fearless children.

Do you dive in course ponds for golf balls at night or do you go down on
    millionaires on astroturf?
The dustbin's suit charmed your Japanese soup ladles like a dog.
You seem to be risking joy in the cuffs of your pants as your millionaire's
    plane goes down in flames,
And you are governess to all and clean the ponds twice for no one.

You walk calmly on graham cracker crusts in boat shoes, but don't you
    dare enter the mosque.
The homosexual rabbis don't know what to say curled up next to the foot
    of your chair,
And the meter-maid, with melted cheese and the most expensive baloney
    money can buy,
Dances on the windowsill of your breezy orgy amorously.

There once was a dormouse with a blowgun who wrote verses to your twat
    by candlelight.
Creeping towards you in the cupboard he burst into flames and died. From
    his flames Japanese cars were born!
The large parts of love are leaning against the doorbell
Of your broker's offices while you rub up against tom boys.

Whatever you came from, the sky or the sheep's meadow, you're an import.
O Beauty my long walker! ingenious tailor of edgeless rayon jumpsuits!
Sit on your sighs, your heavy, murky, heavy, pie-making thighs, I'll get the door
For a car dealer I have always loved but have never met.

A throwback from the sixties or a librarian collecting fines, you're an import.
    Roast beef or Queen of the Australians,

You're an import. Make sure you tear it apart—you'll find money in the
     hem of the curtains.
Twist me in the fireplace my skipper, o my sexless queen!
The universe hides out less frequently the fewer hospitals we approach.

Parfum Exotique

When dual farms, two often one evening, when they closed down Autumn
I was breathing and oh dear if all your red chariots didn't.
I saw a wheel come loose on one and over time sneezes wore us out.
      Zei gezunt.
What or who or who blew wind into your blouse the few and one stepped
      off and held your tongue.

One island was filled with paratroopers. Where Lana Turner gives out
Trees in lots of one tree each only and with baskets of fruits falling down
      the stairs
Dese big fellas, I mean bigger than their own bodies making mincemeat
      out of other players
And the women don't they each looks out beyond the store windows with
      her eyes and faint, pout.

Brought in by the smell of it by the softee pillows of the south seas
I see I volunteer my sight of an harbor complete with volleyball courts and
      marmalade kitties
And an encore performance of all the sleepers or the exhausted and the
      thieves working beneath the boats

During a sale of a great quantity of perfume changing hands. For days dese
      green termaters
Revolved around my head in the open air. I wear no hat but sometimes
      earmuffs and inhale to keep afloat
While the waves try to mix up my soul with the rackety songs of alligators.

XXIII
La Chevalier

O torsion! O mutton-handed justice with a sour tasting throat lozenge!
O belt buckle! O perfume I discarded charged with being too nonchalant!
You're all extras! Filling the pants of the poor with caesar's salad dressing
    in an occluded doorway
While a day's worth of groceries lies sleeping in a WWII-style French armchair.
Die the troubled death of being choked to death in the scissor-hold of some
    six-foot-six Aryan porn starlet like an internationally known moocher!

The languorous one with one-hundred-twenty-two keys and the
    blazing brunette
Carried the bare ass of an internationally known plantain tree climber on
    their shoulders, or the ass of the one who wasn't there, whose
    name fled into the hills
To "DAN'S SHIRT WAREHOUSE: MORE SHIRTS THAN WERE
    EVER OWNED BY ALL THE FOUNDING FATHERS
    COMBINED AND MUCH, MUCH MORE" which could be
    smelled from miles away.
They paused to rub alcohol around the outsides of their mouths believing
    it could turn away bad breath
And shock the world. O wolves who bay for love on the moors! In time
    your pups will leap into baby carriages with their own sour breath.

Newspapers across the sea are found in the larder and woven into my
    clothes, and on the prairies this evening
The long fever of the drunken butcher broke when he discovered the
    temperate zone of the transient deer population.
The one with the powerful hair insisted that she was the trickster in the
    field, that she should be lifted onto men's shoulders!
And there was something to this as well. Her mother was arguing this
    point before the UN Security Council in her blouse,
    internationally known for having woven into it
The masks nuns wear when they're fencing, blue-boy magazines, Tattoo
    from Fantasy Island's hair in flames, and eighty place mats from
    eighty meals served at the dinner theatre version of Aida.

Of almost no import whatsoever, and certainly not worth remembering, is
    the internationally known moan heard down on the docks: "I am a
    petty boar.
A monkey-grinder's first mate. Deck hand on a fishing boat carrying
    perfume cut out of the throats of Hawaiian hoola girls by a cut-
    throat and stored in the cooler.

Where is the cabin boy to sell me his wide-winged bird, that for the love of
        DANNY'S SHIRT WAREHOUSE I might see the glint of golden
        angels through this dank
And open their flower-laden brassieres, to be poured into an embrace of
        certain Glory
And finally the creamy pussy where forgiveness lies for all earlier cold hearts?"

Die with your head plunged between your mama's teats amorous drivers!
The D.A. will never cede this ocean to you or the one we spoke of earlier,
        really known only in the East, aflame
While monks' ghosts stumble through the firmament, subtly queering
        the constellations
And Sara Vaughan sings to save you from your sins. O barbers in
        massage parlors!
Your babies are buried in basements embalmed with comb-cleaner!

Blue horses, makeshift house that we tend to and sweep,
Give me my vice laced up in a corset that promises a redder and still more
        immense creaminess, and sing out
With your sour breath unless the floor boards and bedcovers mix our
        promises underfoot
With what I have tried to fix in the depths of ambassadors confounded hearts:
The hubcaps of Coco Chanel's limousine, the hospital wing bearing their
        names, and the bullfighter, dead in the ring.

Long and tall temporary secretaries?! Always! My hand dabs at my
        cranium, Lord,
Smearing rubies that followed me as I ran from rabid dogs and the
        sapphires that powered their legs.
I lay the several blames for sour breath in this poem on the tea the mostly-
        Hawaiian hoola girl Desiree (née Sir James) prepared!
Didn't our fathers let us jet-ski in a bathtub swearing we'd take our own
        eyes out
Or after walking due west into the sunset should we let the wine do the
        remembering for us?

XXIV

i.

I love you lawyers and your volatile dreams
Crying into flowerpots & into stuffed parrots.
I love also your wide bowls of fruit
And shocking umbrellas plugged into the night.
You pile up your dry cleaning against the wall in the hallway
Separating your brassieres from your large blue shirts.
Move towards me from the clothes horse and clutch onto my ledger
As a murderer holding the throat of his victim, stuffed with fresh basil,
And I will love you with a baseball bat and also with a cruller
Until the refrigerator rings, signaling that ice has been made!

ii.

And I adore the legal vote of nighttime
Like the mouth of a vase that's overflowing. O overzealous taxidermist
I love you so much more than my aunt's house with its bell tower. That
         you make me fruity
And parade me out as an ornament on Men's Night,
My clothes more wrinkle-free than all the boulevards lined up
Separated only by the canals, the strong arms of the blue ocean.

I advance towards the attaque and I wrinkle my astronaut's uniform
Like if I was a corpse, longing for fish-shaped chocolates,
And I do love them. O beat cop with badge and cruller,
Until the golf courses freeze over, you are only as good as the bell!

XXV

You put the universe under your thumb
You bitch! The mood has been torn apart by your cruel donuts.
In order to be the only one with your teeth in the Jujubes
Each day you turned your heart into a rattlesnake.
You eyes light up like a tea shop
You stamp your mark into a river of plum tea
And if the pretty boys don't publish your invitations
You'll leave them with the mark of the prune
And they'll never know the beauty of your boot.

Coffee maker, you shit in my cream!
Trumpet player, you drink up the blood of the world.
Haven't you walked anywhere? how could you not
Have seen in car windows the reflections of your hair?
The ugliness of your hairdo, which you believe ingenious,
Has never gotten you pushed off a dock
But like nature, deserves to be hidden in a cave.
From you I smell fresh breath o woman! o queen of fishing in the rain.
—From you, vile animal, fall the wages of tragedy!

What big teeth you have! How subtle your idiocy!

XXVI
I Said It's Not Marijuana

Strange God, with brown hair like the night,
With the mixed perfume of cantaloupe and Cuban cigars,
Winner of numerous awards, including dinner out of doors,
A saucer of flaming brown rice and the first few minutes past midnight,

I prefer, when incontinent, opium. In the nighttime
The elixir of your kiss or your loving street walkers will do.
When I send my prayers off to you in a caravan
Your gaze follows after with the thieves and the livestock.

Next to your two grand eyes in the soup of the night
Is the singing of demons! They tell me "More poems about flames,"
And "Wrap your arms 'round me like a river nine times,"

But I can't! I'm just a librarian!
Beyond the bristling rapids in the middle of the woods,
Fuming over your book sits the Porcupine!

I Like Tryptophan

Having had his underpants, the Christ-child
Lined up behind the quail eggs on the promenade. *(one choir member
        stopped dancing)*
Long snakes, jugglers, the sacraments *(how come these)*
Floated past. Their batons raised, the riot police danced with the cabbies

And my old mink coat vaporized in the morning light. *(how come after
        every meal with coffee)*
Who could make sense of it all? Two teeth, *(lighting up the frying pan)*
Like those a hound sinks into a rose bush upon returning from a
        pleasure cruise,
Were growing in Penelope's mouth. No one noticed or cared,

Fixing their eyes instead on the miner's florid smile. *(puh-lease don't make)*
He'd eaten a boiled train wreck. *(I give you the world's smallest bonsai)*
Where did the angel learn to play the violin? Tomfoolery *(dese melons stinks)*

Seizes the fish in the quarry. The water is near freezing *(lights and diamonds)*
Like an asteroid near the broom closet. *(Never owned such a splendid rice-
        paddy worker's hat)*
The queen is in the refrigerator, the farmer can't stop laughing. *(*)*

*all jetties

XXVIII
Le Serpent Qui Danse

What I love to see is a big lazy-boy chair
        With your beautiful body in it
Like a bloated stove
        Baking two loaves of bread.

On your enormous hairdo
        There is an acre of perfume.
The sea smells like a moldy bun
        Floating above your head.

Like a fisherman who reveals
        The winds of the morning
My love refuses to put any clothes on
        Because the sky owes her money.

Your eyes, where nothing is revealed
        That is soft or like the sea,
Are two cold young girls filling their mouths
        With gold and with fire.

Upon seeing you walking by
        Beauty abandons itself
Onto the train tracks dancing like a serpent
        Under the weight of a cattle car.

Under the far-away ocean is your caress
        And the head of your child.
Balanced between them is the modesty
        Of a young elephant.

And your body stretches out
        As the last water poured from a vessel
As it rolls against the side of a ship and plunges
        With Jules Verne into the ocean.

Like a walrus floating on its belly near the tip
        Of a grumpy iceberg,
When the water from your mouth is spat out
        Between your teeth

I could drink it as the wine of a handsome woman,
        Loved, and conquered,
A liquid sky that sets apart
        Each of the stars in my heart.

XXIX
Une Charogne

Knock hard on your view the object   symptomatic of farmers or livestock
        This morning in a boat   the quarry.
The water tower after the sentry's watch ended, his fly undone   and quail
        eggs falling forward
        On the blazing wheat fields   or some blue

Throws your hands in the air, commissar   where duck-bills
        Roughly brilliant and swanky   shooting
Open the egg timer handily but the pen broke   all of this a moment
        ago, gone
        His venetian blinds   while perjury

The son of the heir sued the tailor   I suppose. If pennies come through
        the roof
        A man with a letter C, a shark   old hand at it
And surrendered to the hundred   and the marlins fall on the deck
        All of those   isn't worth a powder.

Eating on the ceiling or looking, singing   calling my shale garden
        A man with a letter C, or not   a fluid ounce of
The doughy punter was so   Lovely. She's the gardener
        You and your croutons you   mostly gone.

The red wine idiot drunk bugs   quietly sleeping or burnishing
        Or where sorting   handrails
Soap on the wharves, who's booty   and towels drying on the roof-tops
        The long frosty   among flutists. Among pianists

All of this, cellists came down   made all the difference in November
        Or was it a christmas cruller   strung too tightly
One of them was saying that the body   too roughly while marlins fell
        Lived in secret   she polishes my shoes.

The world draws   She polishes my shoes and zeroes
        A man with a letter C last easter   I keep
Or the headache a bird lives with   lovers of ham hocks locking bumpers
        A cute butt and toes   while no bread leaves

The forms shave themselves away like an ice block   She's asiatic or agrarian
        One buckle left over   losing the battles
On the forgotten toilet paper,   or the pimentos crushed her house
        Only bank notes   nothing but gladiolas

At the back of the roach motel.   stolen, only Ballantine ale, the saviour
        Our registers   calliope. Mr. Shugarth,
He paints elephants the moment   a mongrel dragging away the tent
        The morsel   opinionated or owls

—And why can't you turn on the sink or the tub   the mailbox blown
            down the street
        To this ho   and cinnamon
Starlit mayorality   grazing where she kissed her husband
        Your money,   or good morning

Yes you tell yourself you're the teller seriously   kettles and kettledrums
            or a sidewinder
        Apricots lay   on the football field
When you were called by pigs   Is this boring you? There's more
        Moishe answered your letters by 5 o'clock   duck feathers

So what the o my beautiful ditty   and swallows with tin cans
        Who are you trying to manhandle   posting up
What I'd throw down into the mayhem laughing   while the train filled
        with marlins
        Of my amounts, loves, foxes   and so-and-so who is still talking.

XXX
De Profundis Clamavis

What I'm asking for with such acquiescence is the tongue of the king the
       only one the one that I love is diamonds apostrophes
Bank men or leg breakers around the fountain again. Laughing gut laughs
       falling over the observation deck a sure thing A man irons my
       pants. I kill him.
This is the universe in the morning. Towards your plumb bob the
       horizon shuffles
Or once I swam in the *[one looking over the other one's shoulder two short
       girls in thick heels]* Laynie's story hour or and the blastphemy.

A sun no taxis leaving this house no color or flights leaving below the six
       month mark *[thank you for sitting there you have pleasant breasts and
       now you look good in that jacket although perhaps too business-like]*
And the six other month's martinis Laynie covers the earth
Saying destroy the borders no countries more no new countries but those
       at the poles
—And no one comes up to bat, not even Russians or hair or mineral water.
       Not even wood boys!

Or else I'll step out or her almondine who soup lashes up up and awash!
The cold train wreck of bread and autumn deciding alone if the ceiling or
       the windowpane
And that immense. Night seemed to go on talking and on until your chow
       the highway the viaduct

I lock you up in the bug house to sort out the more vile animals
Who might still separate darks from lights a dachshund but some of them
       are stupid after the beginning of the alphabet
To want to ride on the backs of cattle bank men or leg breakers would at
       least try to give up the thirsted life!

XXXI
The Vampire
for Todd Colby

You, who like a cup of octopus
Dances in my lawyer's dog dish;
You, whose forte is putting together a circus troupe
Of demons, winos, railway men and pensioneers:

Against the breast of your disreputable host
You light a match for your cigarette and set fire to your country home.
—Infamous one to whom I am lying,
Like the charm bracelet around the neck of a dead cat,

Like the juice of a Nazi in a tutu,
Like the bathtub of Ivan the Terrible,
Like all the rats who appear in the subway scene in *The Umbrellas of Cherbourg,*
You're the voice of the spokesperson for a sporting goods store—a sporting
        goods store, that's you!

I quickly open the glove compartment
Of the conquistadores and of Betsy Ross
And I tell your poison feet
To remind me to make sure I lock my door.

At last! The poison and the glove compartment
Have imprisoned you in the basement and said to you
"You haven't dug as much as the student of a loaf of bread
In your bosomy job as the voice of the spokesperson of a sporting goods store

You jackass! In your second movie,
If our stinking efforts pay off,
Your kisses will resuscitate
The cadaver of your vampire!"

XXXI(a)
Lethe
The Lee The/The The The/The The Tea

Come on, *(my heart works for donuts and sourdough)*
I love monsters. *(tigers fallen asleep in low-oxygen air)*
I've always wanted to plunge *(my fingers tremble)*
Into their crinolines *(the lay preacher pays the hospital bill)*

And refill my perfume bottle. *(a hellish trombone crushes)*
Low calorie *(release my neck and wrists from the stockade)*
Breathing apparatuses filter out *(brings in a flower)*
The soft relenting voice of my lover. *(defunct)*

I want to sleep *(sleep beneath a living plum tree and sew)*
On a quiet sea trip. *(the Mafioso's son cuts love in half)*
I'll tally by candlelight *(this song is for the eels)*
Until the police come with a carving knife and cut open *(asserting the
        weight of your beauty)*

The glutton's fat throat. *(it rains appraisals)*
On the couch *(no one visits me in Labrador)*
A forgetful cat burglar *(lives in her bush)*
Pours out kisses, *(and Lethe dances in)*

Delicate *(a man who fell asleep in a dustbin, awoke and found himself on
        the moon)*
Predictions *(commentary on the job market goes)*
And a virgin's change purse. *(the martyr closes the deer's mouth)*
In the attic the supplicant *(don't last forever)*

Sucks on a raccoon *(pouring taffy, mother)*
With no pants on. Cigar smoke *(L. ate his bun)*
Sails in by the valley-full *(until the charming sneeze)*
And the jailer loses his keys. *(it didn't occur to me)*

XXXII

One night in June that I was President of the Concrete Mixing Company
A cadaver came along listening to a dead walkman.
I had bought a cassette of posthumous Luther Vandross recordings
So in bow ties we did the wet twist from the waist down writing letters to
      our private parts.

I am to myself the King of the locals.
My son studies how I shake the vinegar before my frozen army.
His hair will fruitily write his name in his casket once the exterminator is
      done with it
And gives me this post card of the ravine to start my heart up again.

I press on the gas. A high temperature sweat rolls down the forehead of
      the King's corpse
And he pees softly on his feet and on raspberry bushes tucked between the
      black trees
Next to the abandoned train station. You've derailed the flower pots! and
      they're not happy that their rich fronds and stems are down in the
      street spelling out

The name of the storm falling into the cash register for how many nights now?
You are only falling on the hen-house o wicked rain!
Obscuring with your icicles the splendor of my wife's dreamy prune trees.

XXXIII
Dead Letter Office

Lorca, you have fallen asleep with a telephone ringing in your hair
At the foot of a day carved in marble,
And Sr. Lorca, doesn't your halo pour into the Senate's shirt sleeves and
       into its servants' quarters
The labia seen by sailors in their dreams since before the Greeks?

When the rock took the opportunity to lift the lid off the pot to peruse
       the cookings,
And your ass cheeks were accomplied by the soup with a charming
       nonchalance,
Did your heart go fishing for a battery at the bottom of your suitcase
And your Madonnas carry their packagings flowing into the wind for profit?

Your tombstone whispers to me in my waking dreams.
"Take me to be weighed for postage," it says.
But during these grand nights of octopus ink the meter is banished, and
       the scale screams off like a banshee.

You say "The pool players serve you the Queen's ice cream;
Have you never known the pleasures of the morning?"
And the green sea runs its tongue across your neck, as over the glue on an
       expired stamp.

The Chat

Come on then my boat hat chatty talking. Surely Monsignor, a mere morsel
     of them
     Retains the griffons? Your skull shows its age
And all the energy runs out of me the plumber Fred Astaire ten-seven beat
     over yew trees
     In a swordfight at the gate. I'm a mathematician.

Lord that these mine dog fingers should caress Lois as she goes
     Ta-ta falling like summertime from her head and your last Dos Equis
And eating when yer mammy's main senator slips a duplicate going away party
     Yesterday's paper laid on the main course of lecturing exes x's

I see my woman in in a spirit. She her face
     Comes late then laying aim between
Tree huggers and the friends of freon, cooped up together in a gated
     community. Your remarks on father's darts

     And on the Justice of the Peace's only feet mollify my headache
The air inside the submarine until undone laughing at us for smoking
     Swimming behind the novelist while his brown body dives deeper.

XXXV
Fer Yelluh

At the end of eternity is the garden of our hound dog!
He's there now, rolling his eyes dumbly in the terrible jungle,
Knowing from where he's sitting that living on a golf course again would
       be hell.

There is little urine on the flowers he looks over now.
Our hero has sniffed the strange scent of uniform makers and rolled
       around in shit
In the ravine haunted by the ghosts of mailmen's cats.

O the fur on this cur covers an ulcerated heart
Worn down by vengeance shouldered against traitor dogs who pissed on
       his plot.
My dear doggy! Your broken teeth, your gnawed-on ears,
Your paws are callused! Youth will not come to you again,

It has dried up while you ripped apart the carcass of some dead animal.
These yellow stains and this snatch of hair caught on the screen door are
       what's left
To elaborate on your smell and your howl
And how I carried you out to the garden, heavy, with both my arms.

XXXVI
Le Balcon

Madre de dios swinging from the rafters in your pantaloons dear mistress
       my long hairs following April
Or you twisting me through all my pleasures! Or you tucked with my
       homework under your arms
Rocket and climber, a cliff face for days to smooth
Bath or shower warden I see you in the doorway and each arm days, nights.
Madre de dios under the there up ahead and coming down unshorn legs
       exposed after Winter.

These slipping evenings I light your way with braisiers through the forest.
And the slipping nights your bosom! To it, and then I bury my nose the
       hot steam iron the whistling thin or vapid, theirs, the rose scent.
That your scene falls softly onto my train! That your dog bounces onto
       my train!
We've got often have said and in the fruits and vegetables aisle pick out
The slipping evenings from those both among the trees and the
       chauffeur-driven.

That the suns are bursting in these the old evening gowns!
That space itself is nine-tenths of the law! That your dog is a detective a
       secret agent
Rifling through my watch-pocket in search of you, or green, or the queen
       of days without ever leaving bed.
I believe I find a buttered roll some jam there I am again, breathing among the
       fairies and cigarettes, the naiads the dryads, often one of them sings
That the suns are bursting only in these slippers and evening gowns.

Night slipped into the river slowly. Was it would it have been there was
       only one car to crash
And my eyes don't these or we lean onto and we take turns pruning the
       trees in her garden.
And I was a drinker alright. Without his help his hot air balloon o
       sleeplessness! O poison!
And her feet were sleeping with me and don't my hands look the brothers
       of hers?
Night slipped away down south *sans sucre* and all my cars but one weren't
       they in her collision?

I say milk or art became her carried out the smallest happinesses in her dresses
And rewrote or rerolled my old spliff of the ages. Don't she doesn't
       her genome

Drive her back chauffeured to the sea? Don't look, look or look from a
        pleasure boat at her lounging there for hours, beneath us,
Sick of us. That includes her dog so soft
I know the dog house the kennel the cave opens its mouth wide and every
        small dress disappears in an hour!

These slippery sermonizers, these smokers these endless kisses
Are born again Toronto on horseback. They don't they are they finished with
        the waffle-maker they interrupt, legally, our black-face radio show
They come on board and climb up onto old skies will she have to leave
        every solar system for the Rajas?
After she's washed away every holiday she's uncovered with her squadron
        of explorers?
O slippery sermons! O smoking ladies! O endless kibbutzers!

The Possessed
for Shannon Brady

The sun is hidden behind a pancake. Like him,
O crazywoman of my life! you cover yourself with a frozen waffle, burnt
      on one side.
Attention! There is smoke coming from under the crack below the door;
      softly it mumbles, softly it lifts its hat off to dance
And plunges entirely into the mouth of the laundry bag.

I still love you! Even if you are a porter. If you want to today,
Go to the barber and shave your head like a monk;
Your bald pate on the avenue will bring everyone to smile,
And this is a good thing! You are the charming direction-giver, caught in
      the city's gravitational eye!

Light your prune tree with the flame of the lecherous!
Light the desires in the looks of the rusty!
Everything about you is pleasing to me, even more so in the bathroom or
      watering the plants

As softly as you dress when you drive in the black night with your hair
      dyed red.
There isn't one flake of cereal in all my cabinets that doesn't tremble for you,
That doesn't cry out: *O my darling Anti-Christ, je t'adore!*

XXXVIII
Hate Mail

i.

Les Ténèbres

In the tunnels it's earlier than that. Sadly, fifteen bells might ring,
And I'll have to go and face my destiny. Although,
I never could wait longer than fifteen minutes for Red Henry the barber,
So maybe you'll see me there. Once nighttime enters the picture you never
      really can be certain if a moose with Twinkies and fruit pies
Is going to ride into Manhattan with you and the rabbi to visit your friend
      the painter.

More and more lately, I've been forced to walk around waving my hands in
      the air
Chased by a chef with a furious appetite. I find that I've been arriving
      places earlier than I'd intended. I think I'm still taking as long to
      go bowling as I did that time I ate my dog on the subway when I
      was nine.
How I sat through those elongated waits before I'd taken up the habit of
      scrubbing pots on the train
Is a question that should be posed to my ghost in the afterlife. I was
In terror of meeting Princess Grace in full royal regalia then.
I had dreams of knocking over a bottle of Chinese perfume in her path for
      her review in front
Of an on-rushing train, and I'd have to attain total grandeur and spread
      my arms to fly across to the other platform
—Swoop! Brenda tells me the trains are running slowly in memory of my
      beautiful face,
But Grace won't mind. If I'm so late the lightbulb dies, she'll pour oil in
      the lamp.

ii.

The Smoking Lepers

From the top of the key, several honey bees were breathing
With tiny respirators made in Ireland. Nearby, hot lentil soup filled the
      belly of a fat man
Like grain pouring into a silo. At the end of the street a church had fallen
      down on its knees
To sniff the underwear drawer of the muse of forest fire fighters.

A heavy medallion swung around the card shark's neck as he ordered
        macrobiotic food
And shortly, the restaurant keeled over and died.
Since the lepers built a new beautiful body from their old parts
The soup spoon remembered running away with the donut into a field of
        immortal poppies.

Jesus' hair seems bounciest in paintings of the crucifixion,
As though it had spent his life swinging with school girls' laundry in the closet.
One second later, the fry cook and the faun

In nun's habits, with their hair pushed out like a willow trees,
Filled the head of that pure young thing
With stories of four smoke stacks falling over in an earth quake.

iii.

The Card Player
The beautiful card player rubbed his ass against the painter
And being that she had on her lobster claw hat, they vamped to the right
And I don't know what strange stairways the two tripped down
Or what ironing boards they slipped down in the immense and empty park.

Aint it always the case that young girls with marbles in their pussies can sleep
Just about anywhere, rocking like a boat tied to a dock,
Nothing mussing their hair or their clear complexions
And trout tremble all over them in the bordello?

My mama used to tell me that she crawled into bed with an oyster once
And after that he wouldn't stop calling her. Under the sea
Her nudity was as long as a freight train.

In the kissers' mouths of satin there lingers,
Whether you starve it off or brush right up against it,
The graceful climbing of the only child ever burned to death in a fire.

The beautiful card player
The beautiful card player rubbed his ass
for at least a half an hour
because he thought he was Chaucer
and he thought that was what Chaucer should do.
He'd seen it on the side of a bus: Chaucer

rubbing his ass with a pencil eraser.
I like that, he thought.
And in New Jersey they have a special club
dedicated to the worship of the Moose men.
It's no secret, I've seen it.
You can stare in their windows on Pomeroy Avenue
as they do the Sacred Moose-Dance
Throwing their hands high in the air
old and young men alike
kicking their knees up
        going around in a circle, chanting
"Hi-yi-yi-yi— Hi-yi-yi-yi— Moooooop! Moooooop!"
As reportedly, the Moose men did,
In Canadian forests.

iv.

The Portrait

Sickness and Death were sitting at the edge of a fountain smoking a cigarette.
One said, "All the fires that we wave around and shudder
Say to me that Yankee fans are sitting with napkins on their laps under the
        bleachers waiting for supper
To jump up and scare them like a dog that will only drink bottled water."

From one of his back pockets a passing thief brought forth a dictaphone
Saying "Which of these trains will take me to the fashion district? the V?
What stops will it stop at?" "I am afraid my old friend," one replied,
"That there could not be a paler destination." And so the three took to
        drawing with crayons

The portrait of one who, like me, has the face of a camel, and drives a
        dune buggy across the sands alone at night,
And who time has injured with an old spoon.
Each day I wear my frock to some asshole's wedding...

Black assassins of Mr & Mrs. Howl and of art
You will never make me forget Tuesday's
Silky foot in my ear and in my gay rivers!

XXXIX

i.

I give you a lake stocked with flying fish, named after a Spaniard,
A railroad baron actually, who harassed me in the kitchen beneath the cabinets
And made me run the dishwasher one evening while he wrote Cervantes'
        biography.
He could drink a lot of water, especially on a golf course seated atop his
        prize stallion

Named after his aunt, a small photo of whom he kept in a locket, taken
        after her legendary prison stay for between five and seventeen years,
But then he would be very tired. He could lecture endlessly like a typhoon
On that golf course, about his brother and his wife, who he met through a
        Chinese hocus-pocus purveyor
While sleeping in a hammock on a ghost ship.

Between murdering locksmiths and fishing in sinkholes for prizemoney
A justice of the peace tried to sell him his hat, for nothing, and me his
        horse, but he went back to sinkholes instead!
—Which makes you one lucky locksmith I guess, like an hombre whose death
        certificate got lost in the mail on the way to his mother's house!

Anyway, he put one smelly foot on the big book and with a burning glare
All the stupid copywriters waiting for their aunts' throats to be cut at sea
Told him it was you who'd been screaming in the garden every Tuesday,
        waving a big axe, as though you were a grand angel, riding in on
        the front of the bullet train!

ii.

I'm giving up all I've done in green like a shark's fin awash and curtsying
        my man,
As I ship out for hours cement or happily. Whose glue hardened for over
        or suntanning a large or small banana tree
And my fever rose screaming one evening and my cerebellum left the garrison.
Are you a water carrier? Seasonally fervid or the favorite order where
        butterflies underwater via aqueduct

Or don't you can't you recollect? Along the side of the road were fairy tale
        houses or their windows, fronts held up by supporting posts
        though ten men leaned on each to keep them from falling in a
        strong wind

And tired, you my reader. Are you also the typhoon pulling up your socks?
      Three o'clock a hollow belly or lunchtime and a glass of water
The waiter in white. His apron. Less brotherly had few brothers mostly
      sisters and a dog sorcerer with magic bone and phantasmal leash
Asleep at the foot of the clock until Bong! And then we'd climb the
      mountain to recite my poetry.

Enter the marauders the marauders enter through the front door having
      somehow gotten ahold of the key. Somehow while we searched
      the goldfish pond for its bottom with our eyes we'd forgotten
      about that.
Just as And then the bathtub overflowing fell through the ceiling, hot water
      raining on the horse's face My I couldn't say nothing The Mayor
—Oats! Keys! Hombre help me mark the chalk line where his horse
      lies finished.

Fools fill the foothills, lightly. Under their dull disregard or therein the
      serum of insiders
Or those who misunderstood the stampede who opened the door who
      were juggled into the rotation and set out to sea.
Did you spit on those eyes, jaded? Did you spin for the music or for the
      angel riding first car on the zuzz train?

XL
Earth Quake Menu

"Heavens to Murgatroid!" -Snagglepuss

If you're the wind or I'm in need and you won't get off the pay phone
So rock climbers a rock climber goes to sea. And he brings a bar of black
        soap for trouble. This is troubling
Add four rolls to each cookie sheet at sea and the captain breaks his rolls
        traditionally in threes at the captain's table.
The ship pitched frequently and I was sea sick. Those who could vomit
        often in anonymity gathered at the rail speaking only first names

She revealed her place of employment: an error. Monocled or spectacled or
        looking through a periscope
The rock climbers guffaw creamily. Smoothly. Are you still
The wind? A vague attempt to rob me on your part you are an heiress and
        an anthropologist so I am confused.
Please explain. You are about to yell standing up jumping up suddenly

And you drill sergeant, etc. You are about to have sauce on your shirt
As is appropriate with pasta habitués. Your mouth is smeared with sauce.
        Only naturally
My stomach is empty and growl-y Hurrah hurrah for Samson's plaid pants.
        Spikes in shoes

Cowgirl, you leave me alone for New Jersey. Easy to call me, you call me
But we're cheaters. We dance in an Italian restaurant so hiding and
        Hoboken—nobody knows us here. I speak into the telephone
Are you booming overhead thunderclaps and gusts and gales and howls
        and go whipping through the trees.

Two Ton Chair

"Diamonds in the nose. Diamonds in the toes."
-Charles Mingus
Cumbia & Jazz Fusion

Lime demons are out dancing. Ochre footprints on the walls and ceiling.
This morning Kabuki & Noh. A singer flies
To his breakfast. He finds a note attached to his cereal box. A map drawn
       with an obvious error. A policeman
Sings to me. Shove off. You're blocking my reading light. If anyone's
       looking for me, I'll be on

The greens. Horns and bells. Something about
The traffic signal was about to entrance the son
Of the French dairy farmer. The night stepped in. I got up out of my red chair.
I wrote down the hotel room number. Again. Charming.

A coup is put down. It is the softest of coups. Arms open
When you respond elaborately
To a pirate who poisons your blood with the same ink the dictators used to
       sign your death warrant.
Nothing. Peanuts were roasted beforehand.

I was a German pool hustler. Watching films about the sea. I fell
       asleep dancing.
I'm seeking help. I lean towards Italian ice cream.
Los Angeles' hookers make lions roar. Or
Walking to breakfast a feeling came over me.

Breakfast on a moored yacht is for tobogganing to. Boy scouts
Who run their troop in a graceful imitation of the Paris Commune
Pour milk on their Special K. Why? The fencing instructor limps. I look at
       the ass
Of another and take note of the numerous similarities.

O. meets more hookers at Miss Tiki's
Than any other house. We are better liked than the diplomat's
Sons. On helium and anti-depressants I appear sick and broken.
Right this way, sir. Have a look at what I've made: A smokehouse.

XLII

Poa traim driver, qut uor lesses, eu ice a ai
An oi quat re-rore. If ue mut scere it of cours uul
Ren ento a leerer. Alls sabt leerer ac a baths,
A girl and vater. I don't lof eu driver, i sand

Mie asrections to sorn one elns. So get lath. Uur er gun
Ut soncet, a oud treen uvire a ruden oil, a
Distam gursin, a call if a paper arese. Sheul
Cout bideonse on dae lihn ever ule tratst,

Saict Lodis es entelit ul stean and a quoad
Is id a tree. Tame dullet, as u quntelu cosdan
Ur fantomn sbacealoses un endam im dafe an olm.

Son times i jalp op ed i jear ule or id telt er bedles
I pale de bloor. Zie iln ur queem, am ole quuem.
Om ule galsian angel, seatem jere in da dus.

Aunt Viv's Boyfriend Lay Down In Flames

Ils marchent devant moi, ces yeux pleins de lumieres
-"Le Flambeau Vivant"

Walking out of a gutted orphanage these youse strip down to elephant ears
Cunning Angel very balmy day ancient you can do it. The first mountain
I walked out of these divers in more liberal doorways don't sally May freely
Segregates rivers and streams with rocks In May youse theirs the
          Minnesota Twins.

I know me savage I lean on car horn for pigeon shit and lean on car horn
          as an orange ruffy at Fulton Market smacks down on the sidewalk
They their conductors ease misers's steps into the road to boats
Them sing tea time in a mess hall Serve it yours. Severity. Aint cha see a
          liar winding through *la caberna*? Escape
Leaning on the horn for money cash flow error and trained writing obits
          on your sleeve setting fire to Aunt Viv's bo.

Aunt Judy charming. You brilloing Shakespeare alarmingly My deodorant
Can't count the Queens charges her chimneys her brutal aunts cooking
          each day in the open air. This old lady
Rugged. Mayonnaise tinted their them every step Aunt Nancy freely tasted

Those elephant seizures. Tea time. Death. Mortimer looks over focuses the
          evil cave demon, aims
Asters don't do nuthin for the sun nor can any flowers put run away
          trample out the flames

XLIII
A Celle Qui Est Trop Gaie
At least partially for John & Kathy

O good-bye already songbirds heavy-handed or cargo plane
Slanting beneath a pause in my sentence. And below the wisdom of the
      Franklin Mint
A mechanic's rates are smiling outrageous she pushes you and your face droops
Like Nixon's a cold wind falling over at the foot of its easy chair.

Fewer today in tent villages or water towers offices in pink shirts
Or not even never it seems a great distance away a parsec and so we split
      the genes apart in the bathroom
And water shot up, threw out in front of the boat and for days little guys,
      no change,
Hung in the trees cracking wise always finishing or and some flowers.

The Canadian with his hand on your thigh sometimes down in as
      summertime there we were, puffing, huffing
Or where I climbed every day my attorney on my back cargo
A bluebird smell in the air and we paused to smelt our initials
At least down the smokestack my old television

Thus. I would want, if I were a bluejay, one small night
When the hearse develops a tear gas gun or electric shocker
Green enough and late risers wake in pear trees or with raisins
Paused against their door. An avalanche. A stampede without the brutality

That cows or cattle making so much noise getting out of their chairs to join us
Or perhaps an abandoned train or a dead train or tungsten forgiving me
And ribbons in my hair while cargo stands aside, astonished and
      running sneakers
Once blessed but usury rolling by in a cadillac

Whose dress falls around singing acutely its brand-name
Explodes heavy ghost the lawyer throws down his hat
In his folly. Don't I am I at the back of the hat-throwing line?
I have your hat this season smoothly I'm in your dirty cartoon!

Yesterday China was grinning while you and yours flung back black beans
      and tortillas
At least kablouey went the bathroom A cherry bomb A tea cup
In your arms again in lock down. A pause in my luminosity seen through
      the shower curtain
Who where we got down an entire eight ball

And the fisherman's lunch hour and the green duration
On the tent village lying under my dog belly.
So and smoothly a tiny minuscule bird with no real physique to speak of
        perched on a flower
In, as in leaning against the fire plug in the middle of an open field.

What is it are afraid of falling to her quietly, soft?
A traveling salesman sees new lips, her post office
And what's more her father the tractor the horse farmer gets up from
        dinner to answer the door
Invites him for tea "My venison!" "My virile dear!" "My good sir!"

XLIV
Réversibilité

The supermarket and when I walked in you knew me, approved
Over car horns or days and no socks arrive. These mailmen
And the vague tenderness they express after kissing your nuts
In the doorway—where's the dog at a time like this a propeller plane
       going down in the arctic circle—
And isn't there a train a cold train already arriving there languorously?

I bring your uncle a box. Where's the mailman? His debtors roll up in a car
       asking for him.
All along the canals or did I ever think to ask you if maybe perchance
       you'd heard a duck sneezing
Over the rollercoaster before it fell apart on your shoes? It's spooky
I've been looking for a girl like you to push my car into the bog with her lips
But you're washing your hands of me before the organ and you kick down
       all the pedals.

Girl you're full of all the good stuff, d'you know? Anyway, I just got a haircut
And Spring is crippled, but here in your eyes all my many, or the firemen,
       or their dogs
And who couldn't desire a sheet of pancakes or falling off a mountain into
Any old musty palace? Isn't it enough that I own a barge?
Why will you leave me for a botanist? A train leaves from your mouth and
       heads for the hills.

If I'm a bakery, what sort of car does my chef drive?
And the clock is breaking down, ducks eat crumbs and you're behind a
       tree or in the dictionary of
Financial terms under "secrets and oh once there was a boatswain who'd
       already loved his mother and went hunting and shot a holy rabbit."
In your eyes or only a few short miles from here your plane is landing in
       your quiet mouth.
Do you have any idea how many angels that one plane can seat?

Overly simplified by, okay, a good time then or by only and once I had a
       tiny chicken of my own
And it was round or didn't I ever demand of you that you come back up
       out of the pit and wash your hands
And you were only radio static, or only half of a body and half of the body
       of a tree?
But as far as you're concerned, I could never ask you to drive me only to
       walk me, like a priesthood home
And aren't you full already of her, of her swimming or her sweetly singing
       lightly above the streetlamps?

XLV
Confession

"A triumph!"-NY Post

Once if only alone on the bus ozone or softly a woman
    And my arms on her polished railing
Slipped as the governor on the edge of a paper heart a demon.
    All I remember is the pale edge of her cross ball-point pen.

She was late and ate lard. So much for the golden medal against a new breast
    The flat moon sitting on the train
At last solemn the log flume the log jam
    Or if and in Paris I slept in the rustling leaves

Outside of sick-houses. I was singing under pig doors
    The cats passing furtively
The ghost of an ear, or, you wrote me well, a post-card in which you'd
    burned yourself with hot cheeses. The goat
    That followed us reluctantly to church

Was suddenly an intimate in the minister's cabinet. In the library
    She lifted up her skirts the moon passing before the sun midday we
      toasted it with a bottle of claret
Or did you were you the letter-carrier? I'm sorry, ailing singing your postage
    so expensive but my letters won't arrive
    Only my radiant heat-lamp gets to you. Spring

For you. Clear and joyous so explains the fanfare the trumpets
    In the morning jamming your toast or are you is you Lancelot
Your one simple letter on the subject a treatise on bananas a letter they sell
    oddly at market
    And I smack my lips pa-pa. All you are is some lucky nights

Where an infant becomes an auto-mechanic or a wheat hombre. A world
    Where your family has rosy cheeks & rosies their cheeks
And she her ship has already long ago come into port. Days ago.
    A long time ago. The cashier old moaner in a cave or salt mine or
    a secret

Poor angel sea-shell she is singing your letter cries out
    "Who has never broken their nose on this-here bus, a curtain
And for you always a long line at the supermarket with several sorry quail's
    eggs in safari pants
    Find themselves trafficking in isn't it a Coney Island underwater train

That's harder than sitting through having to meet your girl's entire family
        for the first time on the balcony at church
        And if only that was like a trip to the dentist.
Already if the soused dancers fall on me or unlock my refridge with a
        panicked sea-plane
        Coon show magicians open pigs for barbiturates

Whose still-beating hearts soak all monies in the East
        Before the circus tent falls in on its own cracked spine or rural
        boat shoes brought to tea
Jusqu'à ce que l'Oubli les jette dans sa hotte
        As a gift to the poor for eternity!"

I have often evoked a moon a jay bird sitting in a lawn chair comfortable
        As if Lancelot was any match for tennis pros. But looky here,
        guerrilla warrior,
Tennis pros come with all my fer instances or wheat men push the railroad
        engine into church and past the pews
        To the confessional. All I'm asking for is cover fire. Hide me Rick,
        you must hide me.

XLVI
L'Aube Spiritually

Queens chew these, flinging the red and white sunrise
Through the entrance of a society of lineal wrongers.
For the operation of a mistier vinegar,
In the brutal awakening of an angel, she wakes.

From spiritual skies, the inaccessible blue
For the man raving on the terrace like a squid. Again we suffer
How he shoves into this evening a goofier, more dour wardrobe.
So cheer the diesel, it is best to be lucid and purr.

Sure the smoke and debris from these stupid orgies
Weighs like a ton on your memory. And in the clearing, the roses and
            the chairman
Make a mess in front of your eyes, getting bigger and more electrifying to
            no end.

Only blacken the flame in those buggies
Which always conquer your weighty phantoms. Sell barley
To as many of the splendid in this immortal society!

XLVII

The Two Darknesses

Here come two trombone secretaries led by the tiger parade,
Checking for loose change. Singapore aunties on the ledges quaff or earn
       the ancient earbones
As legions of alien perfumeries turn loose upon the atmosphere from vaults,
Valises. My old friend from work's wife's cat does half the licking and sings
       "She's so fine doo-lang doo-lang doo-lang" and then the green
       water, the tiger

Checking for loose change. Singapore aunties on ledges quaff or earn the
       ancient earbones
Left alone in a pond where frogs freeze their mittens off come winter
       crying "Kang the Conqueror, take flight, leave us
Valises!" My old friend from work's wife's cat does half the licking and
       sings "She's so fine doo-lang doo-lang doo-lang" and then the
       green water, the tiger
Is leastly evil, a sad beastie but an ale house once said any small smaller
       flower would bloom again

Left alone in a pond where frogs freeze their mittens off come winter
       crying "Kang the Conqueror, take flight, leave us!"
A soft hearted dog whose hats are forgiving for stone ages the vas deferens
       and our in the night the darkness
Is leastly evil, a sad beastie but an ale house once said any small smaller
       flower would bloom again
Would be less oily, but might not be yer average dancer fleeing Fiji.

A soft hearted dog whose hats are forgiving for stone ages the vas deferens
       and our in the night the darkness
South of where the bill collector passes lit up from within by withdrawing
       all well-dressed tigers
Would be less oily, but might not be yer average dancer fleeing Fiji.
King Louis, you arrive in my soup like an ostrich egg in a pissoir!

The Flask

He lived in a smelly castle, where everyone's mother
Had bad skin. One of them, they say, lived behind glass.
An open tin of cough drops arrived from the Orient one day,
      And thereafter the master plumber grimaced and reached into the crevices
          between his teeth.

In an empty house are several empty closets
Full of the smell of the barn, dusky and dank,
Where sometimes one might find an old flask made in Russia
Jumping around with all the life of a donkey having just woken up

A thousand miles from its barn door. Butterflies at the funeral
Serve fruity drinks quietly in the hospital wing
While the superintendent interrupts a conversation between a sick patient
          and the President's nurse,
Her nails painted turquoise, her lips red, her eyelashes gold.

Here's something that will leave you shocked and electrified,
Swirling in a whirlwind: The nurse's eyes closed at the edge of a cliff
And there she pushed the donkey to his end with both hands,
Onto a secret golf course hidden behind a swamp of human remains.

It was on the terrasse of the club house of that secluded golf course
That Lazarus smelled his laundry in the dryer, fresh on the wind.
He woke one morning to find the ghost of his caddie dancing forth from
          his icebox
In a beat-up old golf cart, but lovely, with "Just Married" written on the back.

Isn't it always the way, that when I know I'm lost in a coat closet
With several other men, with several evil-looking handguns in my
          change purse,
That that's when they want to throw me out and beat me in the head with
          a sad bottle,
Leaving me decrepit, dusty, for sale, abject, with goose eyes, tripped up like
          a soccer player

—Which is how I know I've been down this road before, lovable blackflies!
The sour lemon in your voice and in your diseased sex
Is a talentless poison prepared by angels! The liquor
That ranges through me, reddening my cheeks, it's the beginning of the
          short morning that sets me barking!

XLIX
Le Poison

Even fishermen join the mounting singing the soupy crowd of blowhards
      Cracking a safe over uneven floorboards
And making coffee. Sir, are you certain he said it was allowed
      Or did anyone dare to ask? The red caped wonder man
The chocolate bar hero's assistant The Laundry Man opens the mail
      boxes crouching

Or what if one was only a safe cracker unable to make bread never seen a
      duck headed south
      Along or transfixed by a postage stamp.
However you may fumble in an underwater a bathtub cake a lolling alien
      in tremoring
      And at dinner at beneath a ghostly chandelier at by morning
His bloated breath his bunkies already at sea and catching the wee breezes

Off stern and starboard. Whale spume and all the poisons of a creepy decade
      Dripple down your late tee-shirts
Like if oh man aren't you in a terrible fix and see, here's comes the
      hanging judge
      And did I mention his overdrawn or opium
Pursued by highway, desert raiders with water for their necks and their friends?

Ouch. Could it shall we stroll past she's more ghostly as she's bridges
      An open car door, tea service, uncouth fibbery
Rolls and yodels down her tongue like a waterslide. My ghostly bride returns
      the letter unopened though
      She at least she her chariot holds the cliff edge
Her red brows and lashes open rivers over gravity and edge's tremolo.

L

Ciel Brouillé

On telling me snowsleds or dire news looks that bring rain to a desert
       excommunicado leaving the country in secret
With all oily paperbacks stacked in his orange bag is eastern, or is blue or
       grey or green or is it blue-grey in the version
Alternatively titled *The Bank Clerk Throws a Party?* She revisits the slop
       house by the stand-up train station
And looking up from her chippy glass of icewater the inviolate children
       from her third divorce march out to the beach receipts from a
       spring white sale

You're knocking on my white doors days wash off the beach and there's
       my laundry pops out of the sky there's a tennis pro
Who discovered he could discover the sorcerer behind the Los Angeles
       Lakers' success with circles
When a gypsy twittering over good portraits of anonymous criminals Who
       is the latest and the greatest racket-stringer?
Phony footballs drop on the tops of trees of course the train wakes the
       dispirited dork with his face in the mud

To a reassessment of his wheaty song book You look like sometimes cards
       crawl up your sleeves or these young toughs herd you into another
       postal code
Where the only light is from whatever the sun has left after its memory is
       swept along
And at the end of the sentence, a new sentence suddenly, too resplendent
       so all livestock moves overseas to an island
So hot synthetic fabrics fall churning from the sky in flames!

O farm animals whose uses of danger oversee my seduction by sleeping
       pills a mountaintop I climbed to to do my laundry
Do I love doors in eucalyptus trees or your show horse at free church
       on Sundays
And egg salad or tigers as winter overcomes the urge to stretch its legs
Day traders bending lower than the original Japanese and now coming into
       view the icy gown and the fir tree?

LI
Le Chat

i.

In my cerebellum who says I'm a walker?
Aint it the queen of someone's apartment? Apparently
One beautiful cat, a resident of Fort Dix eats at eight charm school
Or when a small meow dribbles out you can hear a wall being painted.

Aint it so in the woods the forest at least he's lightfooted eats quietly
But what a voice box a supple easy-chair or ground coffee.
She is always reaching up at eight o'clock searching professionally among
        houseplants.
Sailor, it's the singing her charms at eight o'clock who says believe me

That voice box opens locked oysters at eight, fills hollow trunks
In my fondness the most the tiniest broken cup
I fill again. Why does she come into a room skipping, calling me a broken cup
At eight o'clock, her voice fills an ordinary hemlock.

She sleeps through the local train the worst of the evening's maulers
At eight continues to sleep through all the stations. The cups exit
& pour directly the longest phrases.
She naps beneath the swollen depots

At nine he steps out of the house arching his back, opening more than
The pastor's dogs, for example, make their way over to the whorehouse
At eight o'clock. If we ask Blue to roll all mention
Of your singing into her then shiver on the ironing board

Will this the voice-box roll in, twittering mysteries?
A cat in conference out by the fountain, cat mumbling in the dining car
What door on the east opens to bring you silver
Down below or the words appear and vanish banging against nothing,
        only porters?

ii.

Dese yer furr-balls, yer blondies yer brunettes
Somadem'll piss right in yer smokestack so to see soft smokes and only
       one evening
I et a furr-ball soaked in formaldehyde, jus so's I could say I'd had.
First it goes down caressin'ly. Soon yer hungry fer another one.

Dis is how families of lisping *gatos*
Make bad errors in de eyes of de president: In sickness he envisions a tower
And horns blowin' away all his options like de hairs on a keemo patient's
       head. "Son, ah'm on fire" he says.
Could it be he peed in his own vegetable garden? Did he swallow a
       chinese meowler?

When I see dem yelluh, green, well-read cats dat is my heart's aim
I try to run dem over with a golf cart.
Dat way when I back up, dey're much quieter
An' I don' have to keep my guard up against a maimin'.

I can see my stars falling like a ton of cement:
De furr of a purring white feline
Spreadin' out like chlorine gas in de air over a black poker table.
My feet are sunk in it, and ah'm sinking.

LII

Liberate The Forward Thinkers! Freedom For The Straight And Narrow!

You want to wear my raccoon coat, o singer of sea-shells!
The road divider of your beauty gives birth to your youth.
      I want to pinch your bow-tie
Or send my lawn's fence sailing towards the maternity ward.

When you go to ballyhoo the world with a large Burger King soda
You have the effect of a cow-shaped boat with a cargo of the biggest
      Credit card bill and go rolling along
Suavely, singing a doo-wop tune under a parasol during Lent.

On the weight of your revolution and around the lawn on your shoulders,
Your hand rolls out an awning of strange grasses,
      Ending an era of frozen lakes and three-legged elephants
You'd passed by in a sweater, with the telephone judge.

You want to wear my raccoon coat, o singer of sea-shells!
The road divider of your beauty gives birth to your youth.
      I want to pinch your bow-tie
Or send my lawn's fence sailing towards the maternity ward.

The cliff face is rushing towards us pushing an Irish woman's
      chocolate pudding!
The cliff face of the three-legged elephants is a musical ballerina jewelry box
      Never smashed cleanly with a hard loaf of bread
Like the buccaneers drunkenly ripping apart éclairs.

The buccaneer-agitators came armed with rose thorns!
Jewelry box of stories of the secret lives of ducks, full of ribbons and awards
      from bagel competitions,
      Couches, departing giants & gentle sherries
Scurrying along to deliver silver trays to dogs!

When you go to ballyhoo the world with a large Burger King soda
You have the effect of a cow-shaped boat with the cargo of the biggest
      Credit card bill, and go rolling along
Suavely, singing a doo-wop tune under a parasol during Lent.

The noblemen's legs were crushed violently under the buses they were chasing.
The badminton tournament they would have attended blurred, as if looked
      at through blue water,

Like two sorcerers who struck oil
Making a blackbird turn and dance in a deep urn.

Your arms journeying across me like a precocious Hercules
Are the long flat boats laid out to carry late-model packaderms,
Made to cut in half the obstreperous catholic priests,
Bringing the new boot-print of the dancing dog, your new lover and accountant.

On the weight of your revolution and around the lawn on your shoulders,
Your hand rolls out an awning of strange grasses,
Ending an era of frozen lakes and three-legged elephants
You'd passed by in a sweater, with the telephone judge.

LIII
Infielder Never Tasted Life In The Bigs

Me muffled flowering miser
Song of e softly heading out the door
Dallying long enough in, er, the alley behind the sheet music for to listen
    to us together the bagpipes
How you loves to lose the white paper
To lover the muddy the dumplings
Opening the register with a screwdriver on the video camera wheaty
    Alone again Sonny, for miles an oyster
    Of saying to you selling you Brewers tickets, Oysters
For me pouring For mine at least ghostly, Something or aren't don't they
    have charming
    And so mysterious
    Dictographers and traffic lights from trees from eyes
Scrubbed or buggy screaming at screamers queenily demonical in armies

There, at least your horns your fish the sun in tree bowers that phone up
    for beauty
Delightful and lush like a shopping cart, smoothed and eating solids again.

    Damnation the playground lets loose
    The police because your magnifying glass for years
And the dresses hanging from the ceiling or the bedroom shuddering
    The truly rare flowers, where are they?
    Mixed with what lemurs pass for grammar in the road
Or my shoes wrote prison guards in the woodlands, valleys
    Climbing onto expansive platform shoes
    Fountains, mirrors, everywheres consequences
Or if finally I lap danced at your table
    All of your talking lapped up like creams
    And your soul quietly thinner on the ridge
What babies birth includes a recipe for kiss?

La—! Souped up or young birdies on delivery ate your wife in her nightie
Or retired, like a crackded gravy boat, coasting and volunteer mail carrier.

    Look at this surcease of sorrow, birdbrain
    Sleep these cow-waters or cow-boats
Give doesn't it enough oil to the runner is it gibbons going east
    It's what mule traders collect fondly
    Your leastways dry letters begun "Dear Sir…"
Pens or feathers Vienna about or from your hands or bank accounts proliferating

These lay on the couch
Revamping tiny boxing champions
The ducks, the whole city balcony commission
Hyacinths swelling whole the doorway
The world won't vote against it
In a warm reading light

Lastly or oooh! a bird's nest where Abe cordially sips tea
Luxurious like a lion cracker, calls me by name and I leap out of the saucer.

Er Irbralaple

After André Derain's Houses of Parliament At Night

"Looks like magic."
-Ex-Soviet Law Student

Old plue sgee ofor us not nuvr nre. Som of
      Os sie ur qiat et viel te tilgt
Tomrds de tse. Es crenite ur onome? Ur smel ov
      Lecomechun me len hae cild
Cill up vae spaen. Or tu brodo? So me mern fol suf.

And us ved qail ships? Qill eu sent en an arn qlue?
      In le ness er u cool nine ovem ein
Ur old acartament. Ou remts er nu? Do gis mecc ue
      Omcamfourtple? Al mie tine
Veer qald peldu in u. I qalnt nsis aqas ntl ens de hue.

Dis le bele clou heelder, is ior assisst
      Meor bi? I pense ce as d gost clat
Turns sem seap qreen ec oatr eallau. Blues sit
      Scefered abouq. I veol he us slat
Os bild do lice Essesi he es ud rirl salit.

Ae saint pull jeu fran tie qlaoed. A goce
      Levt u ere. Le cloq is rubee au
Talsel dat qapes ufer ue. Sie bildis close
      At amb. Oo saits couv irn dere, xo
Suj, ul pe praon. Iv ae aq a fleet r egli un doce

Leebin in cet eux iellou, n mi bout purrn ou
      Sieen en the dreem de tu corps
Loadins a sen paq er in sis mouts. Explean tsu
      Crain. Es ess seran sletsn abf ss? Aur
Re eu un innocen bixtime tel o purlior blu?

Ib seinc ere ux, au blee ag ur craex, da le pluq r eerl?
      To eis loas eet fam efjes tumars?
Ny shet neers uog ves tors un ae an lous no bearl.
      R le caust mishn ve daum in y mars?
Au litex deet droub ai na ae turlege tau cabxeerl.

Cruts anademel? A rime oe oaris beldess
  Credts die sior. Bin li sun mial
Not am rix is norct oun up lase, nise a mote r dess
  Querren teëreid usd booc sial.
Rasim es oourd. Maa eten bie le darcless.

Ir te plummet blue sdae, gil eao dearc er navn
  Oun tem xpoer te manument
Ur qil eu mast elee sinto qit te uaet te iavn?
  Pla dam sa beti er e bent,
Te sea ial old te cburmed ar er anpiergavn.

Balzac Epilogue
Aat durs Balfap have to rou uid annefin?
  Ae toft se. Larrs a noq un el morchim
Neft cu le rauem. Il lu "Falnen Enerad." Sin
  Ae ruuns ae ourc lee er im.
Anijua, saedtf, vaf r ul doren? Ab u poath in

Te zgie, que er iu qoiin tau remt eur leet an?
  Er maren snae olt rrass te,
Quoste, maec inso ie urse. Mus im je tlax vaie! An-
  Eath te tautr donustone n le
Te xgae tou joud uj le triu sea arn le vais ourzeons!

Checkroom

Ventilators erupt a beetle-browed checkroom of accomplishment,
        converted and reconciliatory!
But the tales in medication mirrors as the medication,
And leans, in ridicule, on my Maltese laboratory
The converted salamander of its accidental laboratory.

—Your medication gasifies existentially on my painting salamander;
The qualification it characterizes, accomplishment, erupts a seventh laboratory
By the gain and the fine drift of the fellow.
Characterize only my checkroom; the backgrounds have mirrored it.

My checkroom is a pentagon familiarized with the checkroom;
Oracles select, oracles tackle, oracles paint the checkrooms there!
—A nondescript pentagon around your nondescript gain...

O background, dinerous fellow of accomplishments, tales veer it!
With your yeoman of the guard of fellows, beetle-browed like fellows,
Characterize these laboratories which ordain the backgrounds.

Song Of Autumn

i.

Now we plunge again into those cold arms;
Good-bye clarity of tennis courts!
I intend to fall with the taste of chocolate and ash in my mouth
As the woods retain the shape of the road.

All of Winter is coming again into my face: cholera, friction, horror,
        forced labor,
And like the sun in a frozen hell
My dog is frozen in a block of ice with her mouth open.

I hear rumours on the wind of each rose bush that freezes and dies,
But my frozen eyelashes don't blink, I say nothing.
My spirit lies down with each bush that succumbs
Under the mouth of a snowbank, indefatigable and deafening.

It seems to me, based on the taste of chocolate that lingers,
That one clue will lead quickly to a whole picture
—But who is it of? Yesterday it was Spring, and here it is: Autumn!
The cold mystery has left on it's way towards us.

ii.

I love in your green eyes the light of green water.
It's a soft beauty, but only yesterday it left me for America.
Now there's nothing, not your love, not your closet, not your ladder,
None of these things to throw me like the sun's rays out onto the ocean.

It's important that you love me, you soft bitch! you remind me of my mother,
Because you pour out gold, because you pour out and sing me to sleep.
I want to take you right where you are sitting; you are softer than
        cigarette smoke
Blown out on an Autumn day couching the sun in its palm.

Marry me! Death awaits us, and she is well read!
O whip me! I would press myself against your generous breasts
And suck you, and eat you white and torrential
In the season of your young ass, and your soft, soft stockings.

LVII
To Santa Claus

I want to build a boat that blinks prettily for you Santa, my maid and waitresses
Phones me in Autumn from far underground to tell me it is fond of my
        derailments
And the primary cause of why there is a black nickle in my breast pocket
Lando Calrissian would polish every monday morning with due regard to
        my doggy's collection of turtleneck sweaters.
One nickle, shiny blue and in the doorway with the mailman, singing
[I think that at this point I would like to go home and drink an entire
        bottle of red wine.]
While you dress yourself. As asses go, yours is more like a statue of the
        Chrysler building than an old sailor's
With a green Polish policeman, I climb the trellis to finish feeding the cats
        another time
Porn star understands the astrophysics rings the glass with a green algae
I make a wicked dog in iron inside your ear. In walks the large man saying
        Let's cool one, cigars
And in the lane of jealousy no more toll house cookies for Santa
The samurai is now the tailor, a manatee, a falcon
The Barbary Coast peels the rind from a gourd and doubles his soup spoons
Doors, locks, handles. A little war. Your charm bracelet makes nurses sick
        at the academy
None of the pearls brocaded into your corn husk sing out for my cowboys
Terrorists in bathrobes seize Clara Barton's chocolate molds. Do you sir,
        freeze your own coins
In Mexico singing out? Do you sir, climb monthly to the doors locks
        handles for ten cents?
To the points on the globe where rocks clash together, where ovaltine is
        served with mallomars with your feet up?
Each dream from the East of a furnace and a bathtub in the same room
        where every figure is white and rose
I take my ferocious dogs demanding respect to play clarinet under the
        liar's club
Of satin, the flag, the numbers your feet humming along the lilies
The door the lock the handle sleep in the day time on the emperor in a
        mole hill a train station
There goes a mole playing fiddle around an old footprint.
If I never can become a pick-pocket a bad foie gras will sing out my our
        gentleman's agreement the grocery store,
The rain falls on the protesting ballerinas at the tail end of a moan like a
        big quarter

I meet the serpent in the train station the doors the locks the handles I'm
          more than entrails
Underneath his talons, I have an affinity for all your fooling around in the
          conductor's car
Queen Victoria and fecundity in rat hats
This monster has all gone flying of henna in his hair and of Bob Cratchet's.
You want the truth from my thinkers, my radar range my old comely
          smokestacks, cigars
Before the tiny car *où* Autumn flourishes the day singing Queen of the cliffs,
Broken insect star where the platypus seeks his reflection painted in blue
I look at you every day with the toad's eyes of fire
And there goes all May's heavy love letters and half-eaten swamp frog babies
Singing out the ironed banjo sends bath oils to stop Marie
From eating the sandwiches she green sent to you from the top of a snowy
          whitecap,
In vapors stacked on top money is pretty orange.

At last, to completely explain the role of Marie in this poem
And to mix up our broken-ness with the Barbary Coast
Up flies your nighttime! September's days fishing the capital
Staten Island sends its regrets. I built a fiery iron September parrot
With many affiliations eaten there goes their madman who won't play
          mah-jong
Presented with the day's most professional findings. Can it cry
I will plant your singings out in an iron dog's pants pocket
In a heavy dog's singing on a loading truck, in a heavy dog's Russian landscape!

LVIII
Post-Midnight Song
À Poppy

Which of you queens and sour faced merchants
Gives strange gaseous policies
To nest in the palm of an angel's hand
Or on the yellow breath of a sorcerer's incantation?

I love you my frivolous toe tapper,
My terrible passion fruit!
With the devotion
Of a priest for his idol.

The dessert and the forest
Arm their cannons with rude bows;
Your head lifts the attitude
Of an ant farm in secret.

On your chair the perfumed army rode
With the author of censorship.
A bracelet was lost the evening
The nymphs played the blues in the warm air.

Ah the filters of strong cigarettes
Blow nearer the vales of your parasol,
And now you know the caress
Which soon will revivify Yule Brenner!

Often an apple,
In your strange and fitful way,
You produce seriously
All the more sure of its bruises.

You cry out to the singers of brown water
With the laugh of a mocking bird
And then you place on top of my heart
An egg as smooth as the moon.

Under the insulters of satin sheets,
Under your charming feet of cheese,
I have met my grandest joy,
My knowledge and my destiny.

My hope for your warring brethren
Is by you illuminated and colored in!
There's an explosion of chariot horses
In my black nights of Siberia.

The Singer

Imagine a dying glance thrown at your luggage
Before you fly to the front lines of the battlefield. The halters
On women and horses wind by, and you think you can tape
Their beauty onto the wall, indifferent of the jarring horsemen.

Have you thoroughly seen the blood red tomatoes
Excited by the assault of wine makers' purple feet?
The Jew in the oil painting is on fire, enjoying the personality
Of a mountain: a sabre-tooth tiger pointing at royal staircases.

Tell the singer! But the soft warfare
Of some charitable ass other than the dead one
Flew its heart into powdery tambourines

Before the supplies of fishing gear fell into his reach.
And her heart's one desire, ravaged by flames,
Poured over with small coins: a reservoir of sea-birds.

LX
Franciscan Launderers

"How novel," your singing television chortles,
"O novelness, my quota of lucidity."
Alone in a room, I heard this through a vacuum cord.

This serious implication
Over feminine dementia
Forever blands the solving of fish mysteries.

If I ever cut hair to benefit the swimmers,
Having gotten drunken with their tea,
What will fall is left in the hands of Galileo.

How many pills will waylay the storm
Turning the handle on my one religion?
Tell me, Deitas.

Come, salute the stars
And kiss my frigid loves...
Suspended in the class of wet birds!

Fish flying to virtue
Will always return to youth;
For this we breed the maze and the riddle.

Where the rodent turns its head, burn it;
Where the earth spins, cherish it;
What falls to the bottom of the sea, find it.

My pretty blond choir,
Sing my lit night song,
Hold up the rooves of these official buildings.

To add nothing to a conversation
But two bawling subversions
Is not a giant offense!

Hurry to me in the lumberjack's circle
O castrated Lorca,
The blue tint of your eyes swimming with the seraphim.

After twin shells you pattern yourself;
The plains curve, and the building escalates
To your fine words, Franciscan lawyer.

A Woman Cried Olé

In a country that smelled of woman's hands
I knew, in a ring of trees all populated
With wide leaves as soft on the eyes as rain,
A woman who cried "¡Olé!" because she had no manners.

Her skin was pale and warm. A brunette enchantress she, she
Danced drunkenly as in a wealthy living room.
She had it going on, and she walked around like a cowboy;
Her hips were filled with tequila and her eyes with confidences.

If you go Madame, to a true country of gloire
'Neath the docks on the Seine, or by the green Loire
Doorbells will ding in the stately manoirs.

Lady, your fire leans over behind the woods' various shadows
Hammering sonnets into the hearts of poets
That you draw through them, into the bottoms of your nights.

Mœsta And Errabunda

Distant cousins or at least the ice cream shop did she involve herself,
    stooping down to examine the blue aggie?
Against her hip the blackness, the ocean rushing up to meet the city
And I turned the car around in the other direction. I didn't want to wear
    the baker's hat in this poem.
The blue, clear marble she'd forever found still sitting in the circle, never tapped
Always missed or often passed over, but what was rolling towards her, her
    mouth agog?

The sea, not the ocean no mistake was her caresser, not the brooks
Or well water brought up by some devil and mailed to her as the sea. The
    blue pirates the blue-green pirates
Enter the room alongside the ocean. A wind is here with music arrives
    with music
And several Frenchmen emerge from a submarine. It is because
Of the sea, how wide is the sea, and she rests against the kitchen counter.

She's gone. Her luggage is gone, the gate awaits the next flight, free
But her mouth is still cold is still cold against the inside of my thigh or the
    rain is cold
And is it true that in the center of the aggie
Her breath is against my thigh as in the meadow again? Several days ago
    she joined the pirates, she slept below their
Luggage. She's gone, a letter from their corsair informs me so.

The sound of your voice against my thigh enters the room. We step
    outside to have a smoke,
Or where a clear blue and we emerge from the swamps, joking,
Or where she whispers and the British navy arrives before April
Or in the full mouth the whole mouth behind the brandied
Her voice in the state room against my thigh and where her two feet
    stood, only smoke!

But before April, before both her feet and for days the pirates invaded
Or she drew maps, trade routes, shanties, kissed me behind the bookcase
And ruffians entered brandishing and behind them the columnists
Wielding broken bottles. What had she left behind? She'd had a box at
    the ballet
But the pirates came in on green feet and the bog was spilling quietly out
    from the fountain.

She, her, I noticed her feet. Then she and I and the judge boarded the
        train shown in this photograph.
I had already felt the East Wind on the insides of my thighs in India and
        in China,
So perhaps when the phone rang a second time the sound of her small
        voice as seen in this photograph
Or again at sea she had a voice like the tines of a silver fork
And I noticed that both her feet had already taken flight, were vanished,
        but still pleased me with their mysteries.

LXIII
The Raven

Angie was saying to me with the woods in her eye
"I want to go back to the cave
And look at the icicles without having to smell your cologne."
So along with the browns of the night

I gave her all my hair,
Some ice cube trays, and the moon was coming towards us
On its belly like a snake
Or like my old best friend David Fausel in a drunken rampage.

When your mother gets mad cos you spilled wine on her mattress
You'll find out why my streets are only so wide
Until night time makes them cold.

Here come ten trees or here come ten dresses
Into your life and into your jeans.
As for me, I just want to climb up onto your face.

LXIV
Sonnet D'Automne

These say to me youse, summer beach chairs open on Friday evening
    holding forth with little change
"Bring me a pitcher of water. How many loves and who or how many
    animals shall live before I finish my pack of cigarettes,
And how many will wash themselves in the sink?" Overtly, the car driver
    brings out pin the tail on the donkey or sing this tune if you know
    it jackass: I've got trout, I've got three alphabets,
And so the door opens. Wider. You have a candelabra. O hello, you must
    be Teddy Roosevelt of on the radar range.

But I don't want to climb the stairs and rescue anyone from the burning
    house mommy!
I want to spend the afternoon in an overheated car pulling a bear claw off
    my bare leg and drive somewheres without flies or gnats.
The milkmaid brings in a black olive. She writes on the blackboard in spats.
I have the requisite passion for making every house's ghostly mailbox homey.

We all loved your memo. The lovers dance among the falling shells;
Their arms blown off, they embrace. Every band member but the violinist
    has died.
The engineer's widow hid at the station house, counting bombs' whistles
    from inside.

Criminals! or are you foresters, wardens? They fall down and don't arise.
    The sea is full of pearls, the shoreline smells
Like me. Isn't it true that the sun is set on automatic?
O my beautiful white one, o my war-torn cold Atlantic.

Sad Stories From The Surface Of The Moon

So sad, the moon dreams of being a movie star, but is paralyzed
In the sky. Only her many cousins
Go out for dessert with paralegals who caress them
Before sleeping along the road, under signs warning "Detour."

The dosage for Saturday's matinee was an avalanche of pills,
So on a deathbed she coughed up a book-length hit of poisons
And sashayed it out near the white eyes of medical experts
Who stood around blue in the face against everything medicine had
        taught, and to hell with it.

When on this globe, in a bird-like limousine,
She lies back, filing down her nails at a rate alarming to the driver's eyes.
The church must bring lunch to this enemy of the *soleil*.

In the crux of her hand she takes a pale alarm clock
And resets it as she wishes. She wishes for a broken pail
To filter out the sea for the lion's eyes of the sun.

Luxembourg's Kitties

for J & J

As all I can say lovers
Don Zimmer's breast resting on the table

The amoureuse fervidly eating and the looking on table-floaters
Liking the sea gulls both theirs lemurs' *mûre saison*
Dese cats pussies and doves, orange fixing the mansion already. What with
Who's coming? Those are frivolous ad-men like such as those like those
   drying out in the stairwell.

I rented a middle class car from a yardbird of the science and the voluptuous
   fast dinosaur
Twist little cherub the silence homework and the homeroom on Monday.
   Tense B.,
The herbals have ways of getting their hair done for their fundamentally
   altered corsairs. Chevrolet
If they might be able to serve you purple-faced, ducking, rolling down
   until I konk you head with tea pot

What sick penitentiary presently on songbook isle the blood of the nobles
   turns at an angle
Some big sphinx's allergies stretched out across the Potomac to a wood
   nymph's retiring home
Where who a wheat farm some of them are on their way and want to hold
   Skylab's tail fin again are dreaming of it actually

Theirs lemurs' reindeers' piles of droppings are out in plain sight she can't
   help but magic
And the parcel is for you is gold you the door you at least half of you is in
   the mink coat again holding Skylab's tail fin again
Working star sleeping on theirs lemurs' prune bushes she wacks foggy in
   the ribcage or who it tickles

LXVII
The Flightless Birds

Under black questions, arguing,
The ostriches hold modern stoves
Though they are strange gods
Darting their red eye. They take pills.

Without reincarnation they hold themselves
Up until a melancholic hour,
Where pressed against an oblique sun
The constellations establish.

Their attitude to the enlisted sage,
That he requires in this world of his cranium
The tumult and the movement;

The ivory man from a passing umber
Always carries the chatting,
Having voluntarily changed his place.

LXVIII
The Pipe

I am the exhaust pipe of my mother's car.
On the tennis court I think of her,
Drowning at the bottom of the river in her coffee cup
And her vagina gave forth a plume of smoke.

When money crumbles in my hands
I blow smoke at the approaching horses
Or I cook dinner
And join my mother, pouring a new driveway.

I dress you and I bill you and you like it
In your mobile home underneath the sea. Blue
Keys lock my mouth in flames

And I roll my R's in a clever speech
That makes your dog happy and growl
At ghosts and at children and at my faded blue jeans.

LXIX
The Muse Is Disgusted But Crippled

On the lamb I threw up on the train. Find me sometimes bringing a horse
        to water.
     Mothers serve the white stars
A barge spilling sunflowers. Sweep up my old signatures.
       I dance a dance in outer space and laugh. I throw out the first pitch
       at tomorrow's Mets game. Aluminum foil.

Poached pears are singing and yesterday they were singing and the pomade
        in your pompadour paused to let a gopher fly by. He's gone gone.
       Like the moon is full of toilet water.
I take the escalator to the pharmacist's. Egyptian boat for the afterlife. Uncle.
       Used cars for sale
       Lined up, hurled at the laundromat.

I hear a vibraphone. It's May. Say good-bye to cars in the left lane.
       The cows are gone. Opening the door to the super's apartment
I let out a breeze from Lebanon. Lebanese breeze. The storm came later
       and his convulsions

       Shook down a lemon tree. Disney World golf course.
I am the bursar. But I haven't got a penny for beer money. My pockets
        blew out. At another time, I was quite a dish. An oval mirror.
       A mirror above the entire fireplace.
       & I'm tired of hearing about his broken down Cuban accent.

LXX
Lectures On Seppuku

So for only one night with nurses and sombreros
Only for the good of my country, before I blacken the tea pot
After or behind what with which you yelled from the brown field. A mule
Buried your company's mirror

Bringing out or the hope chests you drag across the kitchen floor to Hollywood.
Close your eyes and doors on nurses who wither short from brandied diets
Court-ordered and herein lies the difference: a flame a foundry your
      collection of hard-working Her stars
And the viper serving petite-fours.

You enter into an agreement listening for dazed trumpeters leaning or
      dozing against haystacks.
Your if you're in the desert and vote your hand falls off, banging your knee
The lamentable cries of wolves and jewelers

And of the dazed sous-chef burning his tongue on his mother's cooking.
Lazy, shutting his eyes slowly, he has had a bad day. Dazed yard workers
      lobbed bricks
And the comptroller flew off in a rage. Dazed, he walked old and past
      the baklava.

LXXI
Une Gravure Fantastique

This one ghost undercover   having nothing for all your little toilings
Asking the men in the wet cave   camped out in front of all your little cries
The Queen's and the Pope's Geri curls   smells the carnival
No aprons, no running water   he shuffles up the horses
A ghost writes like him   the rose falls, crushing the city.
Who washed himself out in the streets with nasturtiums   like the leper's
          watch falling off with her wrist
While traffic cops made room   they stand toe to toe at the fountain
And fooled the infinite   dangerous shoe.
The cavalier paraded   unsavory cherries flambé
On the fool's. Son of a   that her watch is laced into her brow
Eating in the parking lot, in walks   a prince discovers his house
Lease me a chair in my sinuses   and cold, sand on the horizon
Where gazelles sneeze on on-lookers   the white sun was finished, and
          turned away
A dull history for the lay-person   and siennas and the kids are alright
          making money.

LXXII
Them Dead Joy Or Some Them

Duncan entire grass skirt open house or plainly snails gone
I would steal a cruiser *moi-même*-mine. Once, only paying customers
       opened their knees Football stars box down now
Where I steal a look Hiss to look All stars in a closet My Me Mine Mys old
       birds good Christian missus
And fell asleep in the oop-dee-doo the vestibule, comma. Requiem I
       recommend the *finished* lemonade.

I hate the trumpets and I haven't any trombones
Furthermore: Who among this explorer's club Unlatches the very Bring in
       a broom. Ga-ga almonds
Vitelli and Ross obliquely put it thus: I & animals meow-meow/are better
       in the shop I'm do corkscrews
To signal saliently tooly. Boots on my mind, on on on my more immediate
       lemon carcass

O *vers!* black campground on whose tracks spit out pigtails on a non-
       oriental twenty-three year old and sassy yeux
Seeing what's coming what year at you A Death In The Library & no critics
Sophia Loren I feel your Mae West fill it with my portraiture,

A travelogue meets with adversity and I count my ruin in an alleyway.
       Doctor Nabokov sends Cremora up to their room.
Asia sits on me lap and if still again something the curtain rises silent nite
       torn from your arms
Reimburse my visiting rights mine taking aim and and death permit me
       mine the dead.

LXXIII
De End Is De Hen

De end is de hen I'm letting you know. Dese pale I do not know dese
De van just said it was overdue, forget it, wax or sing towards red, strong arms
A bit more to rain on us, de cliff face aint it see it says tenderly undress in
       de stable, de river
De grand-standing clairvoyant, de open sea, a blood bank where you are
       overdrawn and dese alarums go off in de cemetery: I was only
       deep asleeping.

Letting you know letting you borrow I make a new pair of trousers for
       you, drown ten cents worth
Of colorful birds a storm at sea a thousand leagues and our sisters stuff
       demselves at de table
When mama serves sauces swordfish. Re-animate, revivify dese she's soaped
       and saved once again
And if it's raining let us pump air and resuscitate. Or in waltzes de
       liquor cabinet.

De hen, den is at least I'm all for it and drink it down mouthfuls of sand in
       de bar
Who isn't touching or our evening I find myself dry in de mouth in a tree,
       already I like her
Insistence her mules and fake fingernails and alibis, lies she comes into a
       room with several heads I soon learn.

In May, I drink and battle happy for hours dat dey're dey know my kiss
       and birth or dey get on de train, it's raining and I break a window.
De hen is a voluble voter of de sort dat gets up and leaves de table or gets
       up crying
When it isn't raining but is dark or pouring and always sleeping beneath
       de table.

LXXIV
The Clock Has Fallen

He's of the sort that crumples two bills in his pocket and dangles from a
          chandelier in only a tee-shirt. You can see his penis very easily.
We have neighbors and I've seen a dog or two small little things like
          Scotties barking or howling at a fire engine yesterday
But he's still holding onto the chandelier. A saint, his mouth a saint
Do they sing in their clean hallways or are the lights mostly off do you
          become accustomed to the empty buildings

Ze sky eees blue. Your clock is up against your sternum. Or there below
          your esophagus. I like a goose in the pond it makes me cry
To think of it. It's probably long dead now, how long do they live? On
          bread crumbs My memory, mine.
I've never seen a goose fall over as drunk or ill, it might not be christian or
          revival enough
For the meetings standing up around a table looking at a map

A path between the two mountains.
Who is she that she comes in so late with demands and a blow torch for
          bank robbing
He opens he's a sucker for her.

The bellhop gets no tip that night just a forlorn look with confusion and
          uncertainty because he seemed sincere, he just now before dinner
          must have come from church
I have but outside of a cage a songbird. Put my clothes on over my pyjamas.
Everyone's tired. He's kissing me, at least every night tomorrow night we
          all go out dancing.

LXXV
Spleen

The Historian was killed by home-grown marijuana.
His beautiful valet went to pick up his lady friend anyway.
What was the cause of such heartbreak among these fuddy-duddies?

The wine maker was crying, smoke came out of his mouth
Accompanied by his announcement of the time and his bad breath,
As he'd just swigged an entire bottle of cheap perfume.

I'm trying to think of a book of songs I can tell you all about
Which will upset your digestion like one too many donuts.
The aim of an old poet is to put his finger in the cheese
With the sad look of the Phantom Fry-Cook.

Often, when I'm pissed at the world in general,
I float below the ocean's cold arms in my tiny submarine.
The whitened inhabitants of a thousand leagues below
Know to tip their hats a tea-time, always holding the smoky brims.

LXXVI
Spleen

I've got souvenirs like if I walked a million miles:

A giant marble shattered in a billiard game,
A sea filled with two bullets in it, one filled with a butcher shop, one with
       romance novels,
A prince's pony rolled in eviction notices
And a round cave hidden away like a cervix.
There's a pyramid, another big cave,
A continent's worth of Fozzy Bear imitators
—My apartment's like a cemetery hated by the moon,
So she sends me all her returned mail, and there's a line of postmen at my door
Waiting to charm me with dead letters and unemployment checks.
My bedroom is filled with the plastic yellow roses of Texas.
Where do they get all this outdated shit?
Pink lawyer's suits and waxy lips,
I can't seem to get away from the smell of a thousand bottles of cheap perfume.
Someone has opened another bottle of cheap perfume.

But I've never flown off on a long journey
Where at the end of a cold year
I sat under the apple of my curiosity
And viewed the empty warehouses of the afterworld.
It's just a dream o material world!
I'm sunk, as in granite, buried under satin jackets,
Awash in a desert of hairbrushes and pens
While my Sphinx looks over a nation of Ginsu knives
Not even out of their cartons and thinks it horribly funny
That the crayons I've collected are melting underneath the couch.

LXXVII
Spleen

I'm like the king in a country of geese:
Rich, but impotent; young, and carrying a very old
Bank note; aware that as with all the hems of all the dresses I accidentally
      brush up against,
I'm just as much at war with the dogs as I am with all the other wild beasts.
Nothing's going to lay an egg in my kingdom: not gibbons, not falcons,
And no one's smearing jam on their face on the balcony.
At lunch time, I'd like to sing an ugly song
Straight thru, without any distractions.
If my son so much as turns a page in the book he's reading I'll put him in
      his grave
And throw his girlfriend from the tower.
Where's the toilet in this place?
You little kids might think this is funny
But I'll stuff your guts with oranges until you puke,
Until you've gotten all the romping out of your system.
And singing in the shower I sound like the Roman conquerors,
And didn't they look out at the world and forget what day it was?
No one will ever drive my car so long as I live
And I'll press it on with the last drops of my blood, coolly, into the Styx.

LXXVIII
Spleen

When the sky bays its weight loudly like a closet
On the germinating spirit at the price of long enemies,
And the horizon embraces the whole circle,
Relaying us one black day sadder than nights;

When the Earth is changed under a damp concealment
Where hope, as a slice of lemon
Goes to battle the walls of his timid sickness
And knows the heads to these diving boards;

When the rain lances its immense trainees
From one vast prison imitating barrels,
And a silent people of infamous arraignments
Carry tenderly its filets to the beginning of this crevice;

Clocks suddenly salute with fury
And hurtle towards the sky an affected pitching
Such that those errant spirits without patriotism
Bring to their gender something opinionated.

—And of long billiard cues, without tambourines or music
Slowly defiling in my soul: Hope
Conquered, flows, and the atrocious Anguish, despotized,

On my spine is inclined to plant its black curtains.

LXXIX
Obsession

Big boy you fray me like cathedrals,
You hurl me like the orchids, and in our marauder's hearts,
Chambers of eternal duels where the old railings vibrate,
Respond the echoes from your *De Profundis*.

I have you hair, Ocean! your hands and your somersaults,
My spirit finds them again in you. This smile to the sea
From the fallen man, full of insults and old songs,
I intend it to smile in the immensity of the sea.

Come and please me, o Night! Without these stars
Don't let the light speak a known language.
The vehicle I'm looking for is wide and alive, and the night, and the nude!

But the arms of bridges, have they worked as well
Where we would live, jailed in my eye for miles?
Disparate beings in front of everyday glances...

LXXX
The Ghost Of Cavemen

Good morning spirit, once my love and my lute,
Hope doesn't wear an apron as its garden,
The wind doesn't build itself up! Do you sleep without fear,
The old horse presenting its feet to each beautiful task?

Retire my heart, sleep the heavy dream of giants.

Forbidden, conquered spirit! For you, old soldier,
Love has no ghosts, nor does it have any squabbles;
Cast off your clothes, sing to the spoon and serve soup with a flute!
Pleasures, don't set up camp with your sad heart in bandages once more!

Lovely spring has forgotten its smells!

And Time makes me fatter minute by minute,
Like an enormous snow dropping bodies of thieves.
I go to church in a rounded boat in its roundness,
And I will not search for the tree of a burned down man.

Avalanche, do you want to bring me to the chimney?

LXXXI
Alchemy Of The Doofus

Something came to me in the garden
The other day. I was out walking, and under my feet: Nature!
It was saying to me: September!
I should have replied: Life and Splendor!

Hermes the thief helps me out,
Always looking over my shoulder.
He gives me the same advice he gave to Midas
Who was the suckiest of all alchemists.

For him I've changed gold into iron
And twenty into eleven.
I walked in the fog among barenaked trees

And stumbled across an exquisite corpse,
And there beneath her starry locks
I kissed open her sarcophagus.

LXXXII
Horreur Sympathique
for Shawn-Marie Garrett

Two of Hearts: You stole both my Argonauts helmets Tristan Tzara! Aint
my living room
In a tower commentary enough on falling in the laundry chute?
Which One: I think you think that in your living spirit a donkey a hair
emulsifier
Two: [*sending a letter*] My dentist. Come back and let me in so I can free
up all your cans of tuna.

An old salt: In lovable St. Louis a fortune teller told me I was a hair emulsifier
Two: [*is really Jude the Obscure*] And from some kind of entertainment
I live with murderers and reindeer but no one's stepping on my [*pause*]
    All: O hair emulsifier!
[*chasing in a chariot*] **Two:** [*licking self*] I'm hot! I'm hot! [*throws dice*]
The tuna!

The Sky: See ya! [*ducks down the chimney*] [*pause*] **All at once: Me: Two:**
[*lies down*] My potatoes are all red specials
In you I see mired my a monstrous ordeal congealed in Olive Oyl's organic
eye [*aside*] my my!
Whose: Vat's da poynt ov zis? June's nudes are old and in za lap ov da
devil? [*(optional) sings*] Jimmy crack corn and I don't care/Jimmy
crack corn and I don't care/Jimmy crack corn and I don't care/
[*grabs lectern and rides up the aisle like a hobby horse*] [*still singing*]
Shiggy-shiggy-shiggy-shiggy-shiggy!

[*enter the Corbillards*] **Two:** Mess hall dreamer! Visit
Eat your or flowers' luau garden party lecturers [*enter the Reflet*] **The
Reflet & Two:** Reflective glasses!
Two: Are you inferring or where might monstrous curses separate pleasing
and ponytails?!

The Auto Mechanics
À G.B.J.

I slapped you red in the face singing
Without a mountain in sight like a butcher.
Come on *maman*, we're off to marry the exterminator
In a beautiful car built by poor men.

To make things shorter for the sheiks
I locked up the jail-birds tight as an omelette.
My hope that you would clean the drains
Fell among the black birds as feed.

Bringing a large vessel on a horse's back
—In my heart I know it will burn him up.
The blood of race horses reclines from fatigue
Stopping the gay music of the garage!

I am not a bad musician
In God's own symphony.
Chasing you with that hot fire iron
Did you think I'd offer you a second chance to die?

She's in my voice the old canary
Whose blood could bend a prison's iron bars!
I am the sinister mirror
Who the hungry must stare at as dinner!

I am the plate and the spoon!
I am the game of kneeling!
I am the army in the street,
And the victim of bureaucracy!

In the red heart of the vampire:
One of those abandoned train stations.
In the back are stacked up cabooses eternally
And they will never derail again!

LXXXIV
L'Irrémédiable

i.

Sofa stores don't bring in a fortune there's none to be had
But every day I shave and wash my feet
In a basin. Say to me or you're a drunkard with a taste for fruit
Or aren't you alone and lonely swimming in the pool here at night?

A car accident outside of Fried Chicken Heaven
Must be an earthquake underground to trolls in shoes.
In short, we erect the water fountains in storms,
And phone lines go in while we are sleeping

And illuminate my our rose bed so lambchops or frosty Ozarks
Gather in the sink. I'm all goose-flesh
Coming over the telephone lines and is orange flowers
Is fir trees are these homes for elderly bats or is trees

An unpalatable object in this alley?
Inside your hat, against the silky part the smooth energies, war
Over old corner houses thrusting flames or goofing among the trash cans
In your cat's heart and the television shuts off equally

I spin a dime over here in the boathouse.
She forced down over seventy meatloafs so to conceal the code
She moves overground or the tunnel covers her mouth
With one green hand. Are you scared now? Run!

Atoms are electrically demonstrating bonds are quick
To refuse your packages. I have an Aston Martin a blue angel
I have gloves and am particular. Choose
She walks in with a zebra. Ghostly

And frigid postal officers gather
Under a cookied awning sipping ethanol
Are you Canterbury Tales or Detroit Murder Inc.?
To be telling me or to sleep beside in a trundle bed

Agoraphobia overwhelms us. Nemo is frosty,
In need of hemming, stitching a satellite
Going through the schoolhouse ladies aboard wheatfields toiling
After a moment he's pursuant, runs up into a castle!

ii.
Aston Martin is dusty could I live in it
Other or does Planet of the Apes overrun
Points of interest where shopping liquifies our
Escalator. At the aquarium elevated, vibranty

Cowards! Chimpanzees each interview
Bluffing fell-out crash investigators
Over soups. Whores matching grasslands
With thuggery, lisp astride me as gulls pass!

The Lumberjack's Whore

Lumberjack's whore! What the fuck are you snickering at in your frayed
        housecoat and raggedy slippers,
Counting on your nine fingers the numbers of charges you have left in your
        tube of mace before you tell us "Let's go down into the basement
And put a quarter in the old soft bed and dance around like the drunken
        captain of an oil tanker that has run aground while no one was at
        the helm.
Dig into me as soon and as often as the pilot of a sea plane

Who hears the sound of his turbines dying because his fuel has leaked out
        firing the horizon with a trail of green vapor
Until like a syphilitic who likes to be jerked off with a rabbit pressed up
        against his cock
Every stroke inside of me makes you conceive of recipes for cooking your
        hat, followed by tea and cakes
While some monkey-man goes around with an accordion, collecting pocket
        change with his sassy smile.

Three thousand psychic hotline subscribers per hour leave their dried out
        pocket watches
In the fireplace: Have you forgotten? Tell me again how you came to know
The inner workings of the superintendent's mind. I fall alongside the
        Autumn timber
And I will pump the life out of you with my world of trampolines!

Souviens-toi! Remember! Write a piano concerto! Pull me to your breast as
        your own!
—Mongo tells me he hears oysters singing of our fucking along the
        bottom of the ocean.
These small voices will mumble more songs over their pearls of our follies
        on my trundle bed, but only those forced to walk the gang plank
        will get to hear them!
Damn the fool who steps out off that board before strapping to himself an
        extra diary to write down their lyrics of my conquests!

Have you forgotten that the Weather is an avid gambler
Who wins the fur off the backs of young wolves?! Explain to me how this
        could be legal
In this day and age. I am of the belief that the Night deals him cards
        meant for the pups. Remember this!
Tonto will ring in the hour when God himself arrives to direct traffic

To where the loggers have found an immense and verdant forest worthy of
        them at the end of the ancient world
Where the madam is a mother superior who welcomes them to the
        ultimate whorehouse
Where they will all tell her: It is too late Mother Gatekeeper,
To arrive here we've had to chop down every tree!

TABLEAUX PARISIENS

LXXXVI
Holy Position Of Plant Store

Yes I'm sure there's something ghastly that has me writing to my
        clergymen or to Saint Peter
And after several years of ozone exposure the reply comes to me from overseas.
If this is not what you see or if the clock falls on your tailor and he arrives
        thereafter in the company of a vampire
With their twelve dogs and a small number of important If I look up and
        the wind
And this city has its hands in plain sight on the dashboard approached by a
        fiery light
Oh I'll probably open another bottle another window and float out to the pier
On a tugboat. The broken doors, the central booking station, the empty
And these orange towels. Who's making money off of her dreams while
        she's in the shower?

I open the oboe's case before the porter comes by to clean out my car and
        to see the Rhône through my windows,
That's all. Are you overhead this evening with one of your firemen
Or the water mains crack open the pavement and your dog climbs a
        staircase not to drown?
There isn't anyone crossing the Atlantic tonight. It's too chilly.
My shoes and aren't they pretty and then once over drinks the deputy mayor
Gave me a jar of marmalade. I'll never or maybe only once forget, and
        there were horses at the bottom
When I'd finished it. You leave the party on tip toes and violets
Or an old boat full of chestnuts dances under your fingertips. O palatial
Or shortly I was drinking from a wine barrel and singing about your hair
        and blue movies and blue theaters
I'd broken into in Tripoli. An airline stewardess caught me crying on the
        staircase the balcony
In her bosom her sock drawer. Old older birds are chatting day and night
And O Holy Bingo can't you or is Isabel wrapped in a caftan with the chieftain?
He might be mute, but when it rains his weather vains compete for the
        tenderness of visiting wrens.

Only an ocean can assist me in surgery or the weather forecast. My school
of salmon
And once I was swimming in her bosom in her volkswagen in traffic, the
people nearby
Are you going to ring my doorbell in spring with a bouquet of poloponies?
A cast iron
And then I pull off and drive alone down the highway, liquored up? Or
maybe making my way
As only a passenger could. You bounce over the hillside or here's a store
for crushing atmospheres and crowning celestial bodies.

LXXXVII
I Was Swimming

All pants soldiers now present recapitulate to the march
The prisoners the white cloth the high black boots
An open door or holy now sugary white the straits are overflowing
Onto the eyes and the hollow Now the silent or the showercaps

I never leave. My sorcery won't quit I eat for days on a cargo ship
Or boys' arms small feet toes. The captain is a loudmouth a singer hangs
     out his gauzy under-things on a line.
If you've come here from the underground of Georgia hauling pave stones
If the brown hours of the evening step aside slowly Your horse neighs

A ghost appears a spirit a hurricane attired in roses.
Ever all the brown men all the whispering lovers Your horse noses them.
It's as if the ice cream shop never was. The few sources of information we
     had flee the city
And then an elephant. My skull. August honey

He's here. Who's sitting on my suitcase? I have a question
And doors open a small garden an open shall we say you make me jumpy
     passing in your white sweater?
It is the dry land how to open their shells who is crawling
Beneath the waists of adults towards the liquor cabinet? Stewardesses?

Mouths full of little bullets a palate open at the waist shyly her small belly
The door opens... the dessert tray is rolled in a hired tired violin player
Has his face in the pie. In Rome it seems a brute will push you into sweets
Into all the open. Now a harbor now all the plains.

To Your Russian Aunt Mindy

White women coming around the bend
In a bathrobe and trousers,
Leaving behind a trail of small coins
      Starting at the gangplank,

Pour me a glass of India tea
And let your dead body fall into the cup.
Fill up the cuffs of your shirts with rouge
      And an Asian softness.

You prop open a door gallantly behind me
With a rounded wheel of cheese from the Queen of the Roman Empire.
Her coattails are made of velour
      And her shoes of camembert.

Instead of wearing a tennis shirt
With the superbe leash of a dog
Who follows you and plies you with sausages and coffees
      Held between his paws,

In place of the barmaid's toe shoes,
That for years have enchanted your eyes in the aisles,
On your arm you rest a gold sword
      Used by Dom Delouise twice to cut his own arms off.

The nomads of the North know better than to attach anything to the
        backs of their sleds
With the exception of a volley of fish
They dug out from beneath our sins, shining
      Like your eyes

As they slipped my clothes from me.
Your arms make the motions of prying apart my zipper
And chasing a sheep dog.
      The fingers of the harpsichordist

Ring against the most beautiful vowels
Singing for the master below.
You tee off gallantly and hit a tree.
      You offer to take back these offerings:

The skiing coat everyone was talking about
That you exhibited on the back of a primate;
The peaceful spider plant growing in one of your old boots
        Beneath the staircase;

The janitor's hand-made worker's compensation agreement,
His signature written in costly French red wine;
The repair work you deducted from your taxes;
        The truckload of cold strawberries that are only now ready to eat!

You compute in your ledgers
How much more it would cost to kiss the petals of a flower
And wander off with a law book balanced on your head
        And it comes to... more than a suitcase!

—Depending, you guess,
On what types of old birdshit
You rub into which coffee makers
        In the porter's apartment;

So you decide you're going to loll about in the pig sty
Until twenty-nine lesbian Jewesses
Refuse to put their pubic hair
        —What?! Oh excuse me. You already did all that.

Open a bottle before you go, with your free hand,
For the smoke, for the articles, and tell me about your mother
Who could spin the globe about on the axis of her meager nudity.
        —O Mama, you was be-u-ti-ful!

LXXXIX
The Swan

i.

Laundromat, I think of you. This little sleeve,
Poor and twisted, in the mirror I see spots of green
The immense majesty of your dryers cannot fluff away.
A Chinese woman is thinking for me of who has a big enough faucet

To get the stains of shit out of my fertile armchair
As I carry my laundry home alone.
The old Paris is no more (the form of a city
Changes too quickly, I have broken another heel getting drunk in a motel);

I don't see those old queens touting their broken camp anymore,
Their dry painted pouts and their fits.
The Arab grocery store owners stop up the pipes with greasy rags
And, ever brilliant for the camera, mangled Confucian odes.

The satellite was singing in the garden
About life as a Jew one morning, and the sour sky
Was cold and clear like on Thanksgiving, and slipping towards us through
       the window
Was your sweet mouth and a somber orangutang. In the silence of the morning

A swan who had escaped from the offices of the heads of state
Holding in his feet a piece of concrete sidewalk
While the sun trailed off his white feathers like radio waves
Pressing a dry Russian river onto his tongue as he opened his beak

Came banging nervously
And said in a voice as clear as dog urine in bathwater
"When was the last time you had a bath? Why did you turn against
       your father?"
I could see the mailbox was missing, it had fallen

Towards the sky several times before, like that guy Ovid talks about,
And there, ironically, was the sky, mocking me with its blue,
His feet up, his jaw flapping
—Coming on the dress I'd worn to visit God!

ii.

Paris has change! But none dances in my melon,
No silver in my teeth! Palace nymphs, children in bandages, blocks,
Old cheesemakers, I've grown allergic to them all,
And my chairs remember a time when I had the company of more nurses
            than vultures.

The museums are for kangaroos now, and they've leapt onto my back at
            their first opportunity.
I think now of the enormous swan, with its rubber foot,
Laughing like an exile beneath a lemon tree.
I walked with a hard-on in a ditch, and there I found you

My laundromat, with more brass than a wig-maker's tomb.
Vile beetle, under the hand of the magical troupe of faggots
Baby-sitting the tumbleweeds in your ghostly toupee
Is the vulva's director breathing hellfire onto our ears at last!

I think of the woman who lost her two front teeth in a bakeshop, and so
            she spoke with a lisp
Spitting on my feet on the boulevard, looking entirely like an oil painting
            of Hagar the Horrible.
Those who make hats with the feathers missing dance "Le Freak" better
            than any others,
Banging their asses loudly against the walls of the boiler room.

At five o'clock I forgot something I could not remember
About what Jesus had made in Jamaica! And those who hold back their tears
And let a band play loudly in their heads like a good loaf of bread
—They're immigrants with secret violins of their own hidden away like
            hairy flowers.

In the forest I went on a sexy dancing spree.
An old sow came to me across the plain, snuffling my clothes.
I think now about all the mushrooms we've forgotten on a desert isle,
Of their caps, of when the rain comes... and of Gene Autry's horse.

The Seven Old Ducks

For you, as you get up to change the record.

In the bleach-scrubbed city, the city of plainly dressed ghosts
Where the spectre of the raccoons that made up the soccer player's coat
        stops passers-by for change
Few mysteries are as cool as you washing your dishes in the sink.
A birdbath is found in the back right pocket of an enormous thief.

In the morning I suspect I'll find you having an affair in the street.
A limousine runs over the broomstick left out on the fire escape.
The two doves that oversee foreclosures for foreign banks
Eat the wall paper off the walls of an actor's water closet

And a hot dog vendor gave away his wurst for free. How did your young
        face fill his empty kitchen?
Gloria Gaynor is going around again as I bounce into the bread basket,
Cut into once more by your butter knife in my own bathroom, gypsy lass.
The stove pipe hat that you stole for me from the fruitless halls of dead law

Has all of a sudden become home to an old goose, and the gonorrhea
        pimps strut around me,
Imitating the color of the sky they see on television.
Do you think that seeing my aura is anything like seeing a sea anemone crying?
Without the mechanics of the moon untying my shoelaces while I fall
        asleep with a cigarette in my mouth, in your eyes

I'm just another chocolate candy in the mouth of a French detective. One
        that gets eaten in a car wash is what she's saying with her wine-
        stained feet.
In the service you signed your letters as though you had a cold. The soft
        ice-cream machine
And the Hasidic barber rode alongside you on the back of an ass as you
        descended the cliff face
To visit the only drive-in theatre in the valley, across from the yard of the
        prison for war traitors.

He never could walk you to the voting booths that had been broken down
        in the cornfield. Your crane
Was making a perfect right angle resting on his shoulder,
So the submarine captain unrolled his map of deep-sea mines
As a gift to you before he turned on his heel and went to see the podiatrist.

On all fours an aging Odin cross-examined you about his missing three patés.
In the snow and in the haunted house he tromped about
Slaughtering more and more of the pigs of the psychic bankers,
Mad at the universe he'd stubbed his toe against.

His sons paraded into the living room holding their heads crying "Oh
   vey!": the barber, Abiyoyo, two sea dogs, Loki.
There was no way to tell them apart though. I inferred they'd all been sold
   out of the same womb.
A hundred year old giant, whose glasses broke
Last March under the same feet as wrote down this poem but never knew it

Complains that each time his name is mentioned in infamy, it's been like a
   kick in the ass
Where a giant mechanic drove by with his blinkers on and what could be
   more humiliating than that?
If the car I rent comes with seven geese in the back, minute by minute
That sinister old duck is going to ply his way into the crotches of each!

What old film-house-by-the-way laughs at my inquietude?
And who isn't wearing Sassoon jeans in their brother's walk-in freezer?
Song I heard through the wall while watching my aunt's body deteriorate,
In September you are hiding in the air in the shaftway between my hat and
   the top of my head.

Have I yet, without frowning, looked at the humidifier
As Susie danced across the wood floor, ironing her veil?
Did you ever throw up in Phoenix, having eaten a dinner of pasteles and
   pears and lemonade?
—In May I turn the swans around so they face the funeral pyre.

As exasperating as an ironing board used by two volleyball players at once
Is trying to walk back into your house after you've locked the keys inside,
   and one of your gloves falls into an air vent
And a young boy spills hot chocolate on your leg. Unless Spring has
   already arrived by February to trouble you
For a half-dozen eggs on the steps of Parliament, resting on your shoulders
   a Labrador retriever who howls at the radio

Vehemently, then as your mother raised you to do, you must take him
   away to a labor camp for dogs
Where rainstorms regularly blast the hammers out of the housing of a piano.
My heart is dancing, dancing like an old gibbon in a saloon
Without carpeting, with the King of the Mermen, and without floorboards!

The Little Cities

i.

a.

In de pinched sinuses of de old capital city
Where everyone gots an ugly momma, dere's a contest for magicians
I guess. A really fat man sat on me, almost killing me, fatally.
De other magicians were mostly thinner and more decrepit, but most
        certainly more charming.

Dese monsters dislodged flowery shoes from women in de audience
Whether dey'd had dere small pox vaccinations or were still virgins. Dey'd
        give monster kisses to dere bosoms
Or shake dem upside down til love notes fell from dere pants pockets. For
        de encore dey turned everybody into an ass.
On de underside of dere soupspoons de truth is engraved, and
        embroidered on de underside of dere winter handkerchiefs

Are directions to an on-ramp for de B.Q.E., where you don't gotta scream
        out insults at other motorists through a bullhorn
To merge onto dat rolling fracas in an omnibus.
And on de driver's side, near de ancient Virgin Mary statue mounted on
        dere dashboard:
A small embroidered sock filled with flowers and air fresheners.

b.

Everyone trots out to the trattoria under umbrella to have their marriage
        license shrunk down
Or to see trained seals come forward after brushing their teeth to help out
        the tigers with buckshot in their mouths
Or to dance serpentine, without wanting or voting on who should be the
        ship's captain opening the door and inviting us in. The pavement
        is really blurry, the small sons
Who depend on stealing pennies from Saint Peter's underwear drawer all
        tooting or broken or in cassocks that hang to the knee

Or are the sons of trees. They've got a yellow coffee percolator that ants
        consider too trilobite-friendly.
Louisa's aunt writes to say that the trousers or the trout walking in
        through the dog door are dancing in the nut house tonight!

Aint it them who leapt into the layer cake in search of a little girl's
Car keys while a rat ate crackers from the Russian psychic's turban?

—Have you seen the heads maintenance men are circulating around the
        little cities?
They're pressed up against aborigines while a film of an elephant sitting on
        the childhood me
Crumples my desire for solitude. In the pastry beer hall behind the pastry shop
An easy-going show biz goat captured my attention, and sat on me.

A phantom threw up on Jean Trudeau behind the scoreboard where he ate
        his lunch.
Crossing a pair of streets four militant blackboard designers
Surrounded me on Tuesday cursing the extra wheel on the fragonard's car
Already en route and softly in the sea, with chains wrapped around a new
        bearcat coat.

The least of the magicians, whose meditations surely made a tree sit down
        on me
And the chapel. All I ever expected to hear him say or do was mumble
        discord and dust
And how many times did he have to draw the hoover over his reveries
Laughing into a bottle because he'd sold cadavers for grocery money?

—Say you'll deputize me to resolve the fates of a million car alarms
And I'll spend my days crusading to quiet the city with retired refrigerators
        hurled from the back of a flat-bed semi.
Tell me you are the mysterious janitor from the provinces whose
        ineffable magics
Are captured live on film lowering misfortune's milky ass from above!

ii.
The postman was in love with a defunct pastry chef
And he pressed his thighs together in the capital. "Hats! Don't make my
        soufflé cave in!"
He cried, unaware of who was clutching him. So his excitement blew out
        like birthday candles
As a bus fare collector wrapped eight arms around his flowery bosom.

—All true! But the cheese man was shorter than I'd originally reported,
And it was he who, while making his moves on the sleeping bee-keeper,
Told devotedly of his love for the ailing Louis Pasteur,
A monstrous secret I couldn't keep from yelling to the skies.

The moon loves a pastry chef too, but a much fatter one
Than the one I was talking about earlier, whose gloves collect a fee for
      every sad dream I bore you with
But it was the latter of the two who bought his son a night-light in the
      shape of the Virgin Mary
Which shines in his room like the moon-lit sea while the poor boy cries
      himself to sleep!

iii.

Ah! That airline stewardess is bringing me all these small cities
And one of them, tucked between the others, has the sun going down on
      it as we speak.
The blood in its sky blushes out across its greens
And I realize that the stewardess is banking on me writing all this down.
      From her cart

She pours out the drink of whatever she hears you asking for, or she lifts
      her skirts, or pulls money from her cunt,
But every once and a while she has to slap the hand of some soldier who's
      sticking his nose again in her gardens.
Tell me though, who can sleep through a golden lion leaning in the doorway
Who hasn't written home at least once from an airplane about the love of
      their home town?

She stood there looking at me dryly, as proud and wise as the post office.
The heat advanced on us and we sang out for our lives and carried her
      onto our shoulders,
And her eyes opened up on us as the eyes of an old eagle
And we draped across her marble forehead the laurels she had so long
      been deserving!

iv.

Let me tell you chimneys so I said it to it and the same day a florist
En route to a licorice store a day's journey by vilification said to me
"Mother of brown, doncha know, this courtyard's been a sand box or aint
      it? Out with it!
Don't ever before now some goose lists the names signed up to split us up
      the middle and aint that city life for ya?"

You who seize a football or dispute and fuck you too legless monkey-foot lover
Not only do you remember! Once ivory gone to night court entered
       the building
You insult in the hallway on your way out. Once more, sweet and pungent.
On your clawfoot roulette wheel blackjack table rigged but with fresh cut
       flowers old man lock yer door at will.

Chains and groans and moans recollected from boarding school, brown rat
       eyes in the afternoon peeping out
From your handbag your purse. Let go of your double bass you cut all
       your hamstrings
Meticulous and neurotic. No Sale rang out around you at the depot and
       you fell to your knees in the dust!
Didja cut your penis with bottle glass? A full moon tonight certainly a bad
       omen overflowing flower pots with foxglove and flox.

But me, me who didn't ever have a lion to understand me tenderly with
       big eyes on the land you were surveying.
The eye in the darkness in the quiet French restaurant overseeing the
       mechanical arm. At Easter we dyed any eggs we could find regardless
All those thrown at us we caught. Your father threw rocks from the center
       of his meditation he's a small city
Pouring milk out or following a holiday landing comfortably in a dumpster
       three stories down.

I can see your voluble epaulets your flowers passing us in the onion fields
       where we take our pleasure
Some breeze or nine I eat middle-eastern yogurt dishes I visit—no wait—I
       visit your flowers on days only union members card wielders forget us
The middle one carries himself over into the game of it the flowers are
       caught pressing themselves across your highway!
A small month refills or pauses and says all your cut flowers are upright and
       in transition

In the street! My family! Oceans of sea-cows with generalissimos mounted!
I would make of each sour evening a colonel's fried fish patty by God!
Only were you or did you burn your lowered hands eighty-something in
       the evening
On whose fish weights did the griffin of your frayed housecoat dye the
       wool of your oceans?

The Avenues

Contemplate these my love, they're truly affordable!
Paroled by mannequins, vaguely ridiculous,
Terribles, alone like sleepwalkers
Darting God knows where over the limbs of their globe.

Their eyes, from where divine tinsel is separated,
As if looking at thighs, resting leaves
To the skies. No one ever sees them towards the pavement.
Fish reviewer, their head appetizes.

They walk again into this sickly, infinite night
As the father of eternal silence. O City!
Bending that author of our songs, laughs and burglars,

Prayer for pleasure until this atrocity,
Look! I lead myself as well! But more than your anchor
I say: What are they looking for in the sky, all the avenues?

XCIII
To A Passerby

If I see you on the street
& feel like stopping & saying hello
Then why the fuck shouldn't I?
-Walt Whitman

The streets were paved with sherbert all along the detour we'd be thrown onto.
It'd been a long time since I took small steps with the Devil, that emperor
     of afternoon naps.
A woman passed us with her hand fastened in a wave
And everything dissolved into the white festive colors of an owl's necklace.

Two lawyers with statuesque legs
And I were drinking from a vase and tossing bisquits between our lips
On an oil field. "Look at that woman opening her pots," sneezed a
     German over his accordion.
A stuttering song kept us in our seats placidly until Tuesday.

An éclair... then the night! Fugitive bow ties
Were looking at me from the coffee cart and the cream of the desert spilled
     into my lap.
Did they wish to see me adding my steps to the dance in the milk factory?

Those of you in the maternity wards, it is best to keep ice on your
     crotches! Too late! You've put jam on your ass!
How could I ignore the ambulance's fruits when the tuna tells everyone
     why I'm crying!
O you who love me with your juices! O you who already know!

XCIV
The Squeegee Man

i.
To the body of a fish
Who trains his eye on the rolling dock
Or who keeps up a library for his dead companions
Sleep comes at last, as though cradled in his ancient mommy's arms.

His thick wardrobe falls off around his feet
And the knowledge that below her veil her hair is teased to perfection
Makes it easier to take a slap on the wrist
When he tells her he has fallen in love with the song of the boats.

—Look here you, it sucks when your lover breaks plates around your feet
And calls you names you've never heard before
But is it better to be kissed by the approaching men
On scorching hot days with their squeegees?

ii.
On this terrain that you stumble over
The manhole covers are as resigned as tombstones
And all the effort it takes to stand erect
Asks your muscles to put their hands in their pockets.

What does the fish inside you tell you stranger?
What forecasts of dry dollar bills and what ornate wardrobe
Do you dream of, dead on your feet? And of what fermented
Hand you're holding out as you fill up the gutter?

Would you like (if it's not too steady a fate, laying on
Its gloved hand, proving too clear-headed for you)
To climb up out of these rocks towards your momma,
Even though there's no promise she's waiting at the top of the pile?

What if the universe held its noose around your neck as a caveman holding
        his lover by the hair?
What if everything, even your mother, was dead, and you were back out
        pounding the pavement?

Good God! It's necessary that we put into our minds
In every country on the continent
That the earth is scorching while we dream
And it pushes up its lewd, hot kiss
From below our naked feet.

Le Crepescule Du Matin

Accosted by one hundred three hairbrushes as he was getting off the train,
      our hero
The good detective in the orange coat suffered the rain on his trousers like
      hot coffee.
An octopus had hired him to solve the only crime available to the
      knowledge of the octopus: a soup vendor had lost his gloves
In the Paramount hotel, and letters were blowing across the continent
Like leaves in an Andean village. Some think
My pipe is deeper than my jaw, but they don't know that my heart is the
      home of the only sunset the snowman ever sees.
Tonight, on the golf course, the ghost of Sonny Bono
Tees up for its final game. No shirts, no shoes,
No service and definitely no credit. They'd
Told the Loch Ness Monster and Sasquatch they'd have to get out the
      same thumb as Sonny
When their credit card cancellation notices blew in.
Unlike some fractured establishments, in the clubhouse you can't dance for
      your drinks.
Now for the truth about this poem: It was written by a man with no
      teeth. Through
The screen door I heard him intoning into his jug and transcribed every word.
Across the assembled picnic tables, a cheese sandwich is calling for you.
The tomato is as ripe as the vulvas of the milkmaids
As they wade into the Ganges. Sharecroppers
And farmers in general would like to pick up the thread of our
      conversation where we left off.
It is their stern belief that behind every Tibetan war memorial a demon
      cow is waiting.
If they knew what you told me behind the latrine, well, we'd all be in
      trouble now.
Green flowers and red flowers. Blue and yellow flowers. A white flower. A
      flower that is
Mostly white but whose throat is dark purple.
Do not think I can not see you hiding behind those flowers. I have
      brought you
Something cool to drink, here in our barrio.
You kiss my arm like a motorcade.
You squeeze the contents of a lemon into my vulva. At the top of the
      Eiffel Tower
Our dreams of sewing a house together will finally come alive!

XCVI
The Game
(Poof! You're An Orange Sandwich!)

Floating past your bad sunglasses, the sons of old benchwarmers
Carry paint for the butcher's ceiling. Your eyes call down to your toes:
"Minotaur, make me one of your meagre orange sandwiches.
Chop down a tree covered with crickets, sailors and news reporters, if need be,

But I'm the author of these green verses, and so I'm tapping into the face
       of my right to vote for sandwiches."
The voting booths are colorless machines into which daytime makes no dent
And my fingers twitch with an infernal fever,
Fooling with the wide fish you've seen pulsing in my pants.

Under the hot dog stand on the boardwalk, a pale bell rang out
And subhuman midget queens hurled their fishing lures
Onto the fronts of the ten brassieres of poets who'd had their portraits taken
In Vienna gasping over the bodies of their bloody sisters.

A Chinese violin knocked into Lenore's dinner table turning
My Chevy off the road. Sue paid for Claire's taxi.
In your memo it says that you're also a professional dancer from Langtree,
       Texas. Had I turned
My Chevy accordingly, my psychiatrist would have just sat looking at
       me quietly

—Looking at me as if to say: "John, lap-dancing in the furnace right now
Is the Goddess of Virginia. Laugh at her uni-bra and you'll be drinking tea
       beyond the gate
And every traffic guard will be up in your face
Like the moon descending behind the veil of Earth." Authors of sabotage,

In my heart I am afraid to go to Virginia and show my hands to men.
Currant bushes, with fervor, towards the abyss are bent
And who, my soul-brethren, would prefer to be paid
All the wages of their death among the fir trees of Rappahannock?

A Scary Cab Ride
for earnest church deacons

Bloated auto-mechanic, specializing in the engines of the few Rabbits
        Volkswagen has left on this earth to fall into the wise hands of
        your garage
With a floral bouquet sputtering forth from their exhaust pipes and the
        sound of a Beetle in second gear,
Ella's voice gives your ears a greater challenge. "Why did a woman with
        such a beautiful voice not enter a convent?" you wonder as you
        mix up the ends of a set of jumper cables
And cook two small batteries out behind the garage in a field where
        vagrants sleep, the smoke revealing your error.

Vito is always making vegetable drinks and giving out balloons to the thin,
        well dressed pie-makers
Whose long robes drown out the loud music playing in the garage,
The crullers they bring by and leave on your doorstep before any staff
        members arrive in the morning drier than a pint
Of pom-pom girls' frowns, but as pretty as a flower grown in a
        neighborhood garden.

Linden Larouche swings his key chain around on a ship's deck and
        accidentally brakes your collarbone
Like a Russian mastiff that farts on a rock
But claims that the predicament he is in was laid at his feet by out of
        work clowns
Who have cast funny clothes and shoes aside and are sailing for Scotland
        where they intend to cash in

On versions of Lionel Ritchie songs they've been rehearsing in secret. I
        make a living swallowing the swords
Of an ancient Japanese craftsman known only as "The Crane," making hats
        out of paper flowers
And twisting moles and molemen out of the holes they've dug in the earth
        by grabbing them by their spines with a chilly hand
Or by charming dead Neanderthals out of their blocks of ice so we may see
        the folly of their overdone mode of dress.

Anyone who's ever thought of calling someone over the phone to ask them
        to draw their portrait in miniature,
Who can possibly understand you? Even two lovers so close they can fit
        into one armchair comfortably,

Twisting their legs so it appears as though their bodies are a part of
        the furniture
Say to you that you are like a large storm at sea, but that you keep more
        expensive things in your icebox!

Come over here troublemaker, with that smile you stole from the Hamburgler,
Laughing like a science fiction author, and I'll give you a good look at
        your ears after I smash them with my oak cudgel!
Apparently once again your Aunt Viv's car has smashed
Into a post office box outside my accountant's office last Saturday, while he
        was out playing the ponies. Two to one are the best odds I can
        please you with

On the off chance that you'd like to wager that a portrait of David and Goliath,
        painted in the same style as flames on the tail fins of low riders
Would goad you into chasing down a dump truck's laughing driver
Until you came up alongside the cab of his truck to demand to know how
        it was that the weather he'd picked up in Toronto
Would try today to cool down the furnace of wrath lit up in your bosom.

Swordsmanship whose foots will not falter in spite of my strawberry
        pudding or my faulty engine!
Antique spoon-wielder forever sucking on a bottle of raspberry beer!
Coming over the garden wall with your sword pulled out of him, but then
        returned to its place, is your seamstress on time for an appointment
I saw you make, though you knew you'd not be able to keep it. You'd be
        too busy hurling epitaphs at border-crossers.

Girl afraid, I looked up the shoes you laid before our Thanksgiving turkey
        in the handbook of administrative assistantships,
And found no worthy introduction to them after four hours of research
In a sacred motel within shouting range of the train station.
What we should lay at the feet of the birds we cook the rest of the year hasn't
        been made any clearer either by this most colorful investigation

Whose legwork was full of reading horrible letters written by inconsolate
        illiterates, penny-pinching oracles wandering through wheat fields
Trying to expel the vertigo laid on them by dancers who edge the rooftops
        of local apartment buildings without caution or life insurance
But won't stop for a minute to contemplate why any phrase beginning
        with "Like the sands through an hourglass…" doesn't drive
        Americans in the Maritimes to revolt!
The eternal smile of the twenty-two teeth.

For instance, who never cut open their arm on a spine of glass sticking out
   from a window they were washing
And who has never sucked up the blood from this cut and fainted and
   tumbled down a flight of stairs in the arms of a beautiful
Lump on the head, or a broken leg, or even lost an eye or an ear and been
   mad about it later and gone 'round with a bee in their bonnet
   refusing to vacate a public toilet on the streets of Paris?
Who hasn't made the unappetizing climb up the hill to kill the head priest
   of Sacre Coeur

But upon getting there had to let out a howl like a dog because *he* had no
   nose, and one of his eyes fell out at the table over dinner
Because when the dancers gaily climbed the steps to the roof of an office
   building he told them
"Airplane drivers, you should pay the air for the grey acts of deputized
   ditch-diggers red-cheeked on amyl nitrate
You mail every day to the dead! O musical floor washers!

Germanized, androgynous flirts! Dandies with faces that have been pushed
   through plate glass!
Deer carcasses glazed in ice, tied to the hoods of cars with the lace of
   cherubim's lingerie!
The branch manager of the biggest library ever deals out cards without fear
   on the hood of the cab driving me home,
Just as you've taught him to on days when too much rain or fog made
   traveling upriver in a canoe

To the frozen quays where the senator hoards the boats he's stolen with
   the aid of a magic potion that makes him appear as though he
   were the Duke of Orange
Which gets him in easily to the best of the yacht clubs on nights when
   barbecue and gossip and talk of who's fucking the tennis pro turn
   all eyes
Towards a troupe on stage who perform the jingles from everyone's favorite
   commercials in the style of Bob Dylan *(Clap onnn/Clap offf)*
Without instruments while a force from beyond, which they cannot see,
   shakes down the night, gunning a black trombone.

In every air-conditioned laundromat, unless he's busy getting the sun
   soused, Death is admiring you like a tea-kettle.
Your aunt opens a faucet and turns her body to face Zion at tea time, and
   then sets out some crackers and imagines the day of the Rapture,
And the tennis pro, with the wind in his hair, like you, moves into the
   smoking section of the mirrored bar
To watch a rainstorm rise off of a shirt he dry-cleaned himself!"

I Love My Answering Machine

I don't ever want to wait for soft money to see you passing me in the street
 or stop to tie your shoelaces,
I'm lonely, my song's in a breezy vault, and what I prefer is simply an island
Hanging above a quartet of singers. I lent you
The only time I had available for walking secretly behind enemy lines. Your
 look broke and your look broke an entire fountain

When you and I built a temple together. All the few gasses that color
 our money
Or push you off the bridge are climbing the trellis presently. There, that's
 no way to look
Or the torches are reflected in your glasses
And your eyes have their own addresses.

I might say to myself: What if she's beautiful? And bizarrely as fresh as cream?
What if I remember an enormous dog and fall under the wheels of a tour bus?
What if my answering machine had lips like hers and she was royalty, and her
 royal nephews responding to the metric system fell from a peach tree?
Is it all blackness and walls around no shelter or where do we go if a
 bomb drops?

Are you the fruit of autumn the penny-saver swears by?
Are you the fun-loving, beer-swigging attendant whose cuddly koo-koo-ka-
 choos bring tears to my eyes?
Isn't it your perfume that has me dreaming of oil fires over oaisises
While a hand reaches up from the basement touching my naked calf? Or
 are you just the buttonhole guy?

I know that Stevie Wonder will never record another album as melancholy
 and triumphant as *Fullfillingness' First Finale*
But who will reel backwards and point beyond the schoolrooms to a
 hidden ruby mine, the locksmith?
With his buttery handwriting, joyless? All his jewelry is homespun.
They're too quick for us. They're wider than your mother's bedroom.
 Oceans, birds,

Maids won't fill in the gap between our steps and theirs. I was enjoying a
 lap dance
At the end of a long day with my uncle & his locksmith. Do you want to
 know the truth?
All that mattered to me, Betsy, was that wherever you tied your pants on
You drew the curtains and shut the door and that I was in the room. I
 adore the bows you tie.

XCIX

Jenny's steps forget what she's seen already flowers or cut flowers or
      already seven o'clock
In our white custard house. Small but on the train, writing
Her poem on today's menu of blue plate specials and already full, the train
      whistle, her delta
All waltzing or a bouquet arrives for the chef and waits in the kitchen.
      How much for each? If they could only remember or still knew
And when fewer cheered and when fewer asked directions and when more
      leaves rustled and the spelling bee champion came forward
Unlocking the door at last. Dear Evictee, can you wash your hands in the
      life on the rails? Where do you brush your hair? Are you wiser now
Than you once seemed, painting with oils in a bus terminal or turning
      green? The sky is preoccupied
With wizards Has it stopped snowing Is the princess in the North Sea? The
      long and silent
Do-overs, the pre-painting, how I had to have my parts fit on again. For
      the most part her bateaux bounced off the water and her scarf
Covered her nose. A tugboat hired to pull through the wind and the horse
      riders arrived at the edge dressed again in green.

C

The dog man's foot servant   jumped out of the loose jail
And who sleeps under the hotel staircase   as an humbled pet flea
We'd better become pudding-heads   carrying several flowers to calm
The dead, the poor dead   has several big welfare checks
And when October's soufflé   eating my cherished arboretum
His son was out selling red cantaloupes   on tour with the Marlboro
      Man's tackle box
And fresh breath, he dove into the traveler's pockets   living between
      burgled countess' baubles
Sleeping on the doormat in the moon base when the fountain started up
      warmly in the drapes
Electric tennis for divorcees meant   songs you mistake for steel
That with no partner to read with   the German crow reads without smiling
Old windshield wipers, rain shoes   made sicker by the soap
They could see the fry cook's knees   ice age down by the river
And the bicycle's color was anything but   Martin's infamous relatives
Rembrandt's lovely lamb   who swing down from the bumper of the car
Lobster bisque in the bushes still drizzling   and sing if the reservoir
Calmly on the ferris wheel   I washed my ears from this chair
If on some bluish night   and froze in December
I find myself wrapped in tapestry   one came to my room
In my grave when the fountain comes on   one of his sons was always
      drunk and eating a hairnet
Cover the elephant   one of his sons sank in the monk's laundromat
What porridge alone cannot tell me   Asia Carrera Pia Zadora
I came all this way to watch the trees crying   decided to send Father
      Pierre to a quiz show.

CI
Brooms And Tears

O end of Autumn, Winter, printings trampled and bold,
Dreaming seasons! I love you and you leave
Envelopes against my heart and my crevice
Of tinsel and vapor, addressed towards a vague falling.

In this grand plain where Autumn freezes its humour,
Or by the long nights where the tongue is enrolled,
My best ass, which at times may renovate the tide,
Forgets largely the sicknesses of his enterprise.

Nothing is quieter than a heart plain to funereal things
And from these long hours descends the primitive.
O *blafardes saisons*, queens of our climates:

That, the permanent aspect of your pale arms.
—If it isn't this, but a night without a moon, two by two
Dream out the hat-maker on a hazardous book.

CII
Two Buddhist Monks Gunned Their Motorcycles/Rêve Parisien

i.

While two-stepping poorly in the hallway
A telephone I'd assumed was broken trembled.
The next morning I could still see it ringing,
Softly. On the other end of the line was a lion waiting to lick my bones, softly.

Some may say that the letter L can lift a half empty cup of tea,
But I've only ever seen one man in an expensive hat
Empty his coffee cup just by lowering his spectacles.
A giant zucchini

And a painter have set fire to my genius brain
And now I only want to taste at the back of my palate
The uninvited monotony
Of Mutual of Omaha dumbwaiters, Marlboros and rent checks.

You might find me singing on the stairway or in the lobby of your
        building, love.
Mine is a state of infinite palsy-walsy-ness,
Full of the baths and the showers we take together
And when Tom bangs his knees on the doormat in front of the hairdressers

And contract killers with poor vision
Come riding up stoked on crystal meth
You will see that my suspenders still overlap my blue blouse.
Add these things together on the side of an aluminum hospital wall

And it is not the names of trees but of colonists
That will lay down on your tongue. Sleepily turn them over.
Where do gigantic naiads get off
Trying to look like a woman walking into a room to see herself in a mirror?

Their watery necks, covered in pancake, are still blue;
Between their thighs of red and green
Dangle a million rooms
Where every green wave finds its coffin.

My tea cup was broken by a rock thrown anonymously
As I marched past in the parade of playing cards. My tea cup

Was memorialized almost immediately in a giant block of ice sculpted with
        a blow dryer—so large you could
Pour the entirety of the Lincoln Memorial reflecting pool into it and
        there'd still be room for the tea!

Shoe sales scientists and tax form handlers
Of the Ganges, in the firmament
The litterbug makes his way across the backs of the paychecks
Of comic book heroes, bakers and baseball stars.

Architect of the Staten Island Ferry's dining area,
I made, at the lip of a volcano,
With a pig who digs for cherry pits,
A passage for an ocean class garbage barge

And now, here to hoot my horn, is the mother of the color of the night.
Her wheat makes love to both genders with wide-eyed clarity.
The rain runs down the inside of her thigh to kiss her foot
As she dances in her stockings in a men's bathroom stall without shame.

Dry star of millionaires, voided clothes
Of the desolate, a letter fell at the foot of the sales lady
Illuminating her large toeless pumps
That few had seen shine personally.

The witness to the movements of Virginia's rivers
Was planning a hideous and wicked new voting booth
With hot oil pouring on your nose, and lazer rays re-melting your crown
And sea birds nesting silently in your hair.

ii.
Upon finding my eyes full of flames again
I saw the horror of my toadies
And smelled, upon re-entering my donkey,
The point of marauders' saucy remarks.

The pendulum swinging over the funeral of non-native speakers of English
Sung out brutally at noon,
And the sky sent down its arms
To the saddened Earth, filled with gourds.

CIII
Le Crepescule Du Soir

A cheese sandwich was calling me from across the boulevards, but when I
        climbed through the backyards to speak with it
It had gone. O how I had wanted it for my very own.
Here, in the front of my pants, I had devised a pocket for it
So I might press it to my vulva as I chastised our train's porter. An absence
        of ambition
Must not hang tight on the curves of the rails, it must not
Call me at four in the morning and replay for me over the phone
The sound of the bell tower tolling and bats breaking their noses at four a.m.
        Do not
Call me with your hamburger orders, demands for french fries and crab cakes
To come flowing out of the empty horn of Dexter Gordon. Not 2 in
        the afternoon,
Not four in the afternoon. Not 8:10. A cheese
Sandwich was calling to me across the wen of her breast, and though
        preoccupied,
I made time for it, and this is how
I've come to land in the gutter. I thought my Italian shoes would ever
        spare me from the paradigm
Of losing my shirt and camels in an alleyway of the underworld. You knew
A love song once. Once you knew several
Love songs. Now you know none. As fiercely as the public
And the law makers pounded their fists into your back
You never let them leak again from your mouth or anus. Did you hear
The cheese sandwich S., howling to you above the air raid sirens of San Diego?
Did you hear the siren pressed up against the bread, her ass more
        comfortable
Than any wicker chair? Her voice and teeth astound the earth
With flowers. From the Kremlin
A cheese sandwich was singing to me, and so I directed the driver of my cessna
To veer in that direction. When I arose
From the wreckage in a field of Vessuvian greenery, I knew the dues I'd
Found in the hollow of his tin drum were only passing fancy. A word with you
If I may. You've read, I presume, Rudyard Kipling's *The Jungle Book*. In
        the hospital
I came across a prostitute who is crushing that book between her legs. A
        small boy
Lit a candle by his window so the song would find it's way home to him. She
Bites down on the snake, and we both
Know that that's no good. My vulva

Does not approve. A young boy falls asleep with his hand against the
        windowsill. An elephant
In his dream is doing somersaults in Washington Square Park. You told me
I should not expect you for tea, but there you were, with the cheese
        sandwich in your hand. The calendar
Since has broken, my watch spits out its batteries. Across the dales I could
        hear the terror in her voice. O cheese sandwich
That cries out in the night, I hear your dismay
And I am coming to rescue you at last!

Le Vin

CIV
L'Ame Du Vin

One evening when I was ancient and clapping hands enough to call out
    from among the bottle necks:
"Homey, if only old green and then you'll push me down to the antique wagon
Someone shall leave me a warren-full of green and circular saws or maybe
You'll sing and on a penal colony light and a light jacket tied around your waist.

I was a bank teller with knowledge. Mixed up by earthquakiness his sister
    fed the cat milk again and I alone was left to curse in the cellar
Driving a nail through her foot or she brought me a jacket. It was nice and
    new and the collar was trimmed with an oil fire
Ravaging a bird sanctuary. Let's speak of my life, of how down below a
    manhole cover I broke an ankle and ate my only brother
But I was a banker with an intimate knowledge of the Gold Coast and my
    pockets, he emptied my pockets producing dumplings.

What then if driving off and someone pushes someone off a cliff—you—
And didn't you have a nice jacket as you bounced on the rocks below?
    Your shoes are stolen,
Long distance carriers emerge from the men's room and *they* fall off the cliff
Or me, I see better when they met me in the desert propping up a cokes
    machine. You're a fucking caveman.

Is it your intention to steal all the bank notes to steal all the notes? Maybe
    you're singing on Waffle Sunday
In the men's room where an oil fire where gazelles and where I stop to
    check the cardinal's pulse.
Unless you could, and could you knock over the table with your hands
    bound together or could you manage
And then once you lit my funeral pyre but I was calf-roping in Texas.

A light in your eyes, a hungry woman in the ravine behind your house.
A sporty little car fills with gerrymandering, with a Hoover Dam or with

Me, a knowledgeable bank teller and I move freely from or at least you are
        complete, my riverbank,
All I ask in return is that you carry home my kittens.

I'm falling into your gazpacho.
Each crumb of your loaf that reaches my skin fertilizes me.
For each person waiting in line for our love there's a lap dog swimming
Across the moat from the jail towards old green, and do you have you
        something to say before you fly off in arrears?"

You Step Outside Of The Week's Shuffling Yesses
for Shawn-Marie Garrett

Sometimes when I think of you drinking red wine from a clear glass the
       room is shaken
Or I've forgotten to open the flue above the fireplace and a bat flies down
       into the flames who would have otherwise beaten me at a contest
       of making dark towers out of playing cards like a greenhorn,
Which I am at heart, have been ever since, like a chimney sweep, you sic'd
       your hell-hounds on me, their fangs
Making me cry out absurdly, though only the apes were left in the forest to
       hear my yellow voice.

I have seen you stuffing cotton balls into chocolates at the factory quite
       frequently, tilting your head to one side like a wild boar
In a butoh performance, and I'm fully aware that you'd stand me up
       against a wall before a firing squad for my poetry
And though I don't want you to lose any part of your decaying vegetable
       frown, these facts
Are like the white flour that falls from your wig onto your epaulets at the
       end of a glorious film.

Prawns cannot surmount you. Dictaphones waste days in submarines trying
       to find a way to be your call girl.
The ass of my *pantalones* was torn open by army ants trying to fund your
       refugee relief projects
And beneath the stars a sow talks from the school superintendent's
       office phone
Sending out your curriculum vitae to day-traders to convince them of
       your virtue.

Yes, harlots in motorcycle jack boots spit forth gems when they approach
       your name smiling. On the average,
Mollusks travel farther and suffer greater hardships trying to guess your age
As the winds lift you up by your feet on your way to the grocery. You
       know that eating raw lumber when there're no aperitifs to be
       found among the rubble of the collapsed house
Is a sure-fire way to get upchucking in a hurry. "Confucius says," you say,
       "Most Parisians

Will come back to smoke here again, once the smell of the smokestack is gone."
Swiss processor-chip makers toast you with champagne from the
       battlements, bleaching

Their mustaches as you drape yourself over the old landscape.
It is all Lebanese florists can do not to have their elephants fall down in
    front of your navel

And dress up like a seedless grape, bobbing in the Indian Ocean. Only in
    you does the magpie
Drive an ambulance and write letters from the Eiffel Tower to a foreign
    aunt of an illuminated orgy
Where speech makers and soft-spoken matadors help Bierce Ambrose
Carry in a leggy stewardess from LaGuardia. Even people who think that
    the harbor

Is what makes travelers antsy to loom over an animating studio freely espouse
Red wine rolling over your dolorous tongue and onto your blouse
    and cigarettes,
Because the goosier you become when recounting your exploits
And the more regal, the better all these fake dons can see that yours is the
    dance of the King of Leverage.

Pull the chewing gum from your hair and let the dogs run through your
    heart to line up for soup at the bursar's office,
Of all the old-time bank robbers who paint with a stick of margarine in silence,
You alone touch the dead dare-devil in me, who having reached the end of
    his last bottle
Had his bar tab calculated, got up onto his feet, and ran screaming out
    onto the dance floor!

Leaving The Spanish Admiral

My woman is East   thrown out of a Swiss library!
I put the dog out   all my fish. Korean
The gold line. J's rent   looks in the sand for a hoof print
Her cries remove my shirt   sun on the wheat.

In Autumn, quinine   I am on-time
The water comes from a cave   the Spanish Admiral...
Our plane shattered   none of the wheat talking to itself
So I had my boobs done   becoming devilish lovers!

The horrible southern dry   who wrote me a check
Humidifier. The butler draws   to open up my luggage
Three Musketeers on the sofa   in a queen. Put a tenner
The family plot   —it can't be my poor dear

I threw my first face mask   fond of swordfish feet
And I sang in a musical   pushed on her
Permanent tousled   at the edge of the fleet
—Prisoners remember   yes I am a leprechaun!

In Namibia   ten ermine dresses
Don't run at a steam engine   have you strung the deer up
April. New   the treaty arranger
Oboe music entered the room   about the time we changed addresses

Jim was crying on the farmland   Leanne tore up the contract
Lashes, surely. And for my   on a road close to the house
Elephant! Foal   foolish creature!
Our sumptuous   toes adding lemons to the focus on

Once again she   about your joviality
Added Croatian sums   sleeping fish! Eat me
I sat on top of Amy more than   ! there's a reason why
I told the pasta machine: climb   comes from a fiefdom!

An empty permit   doesn't add up. One seal
Cheese on these ivories   Agnes' stupidity
Do the trees dance and sing   six nights of auctions auctions auctions
Loving in secret your wine   and only one lint brush?

And this crappy mule   the fortress
Handsome mothers   answering machine
Hardly ever, not in Spring   spring nor winter
Not selling me a dead lamb   love's green table

With a bus full of seniors   goes by her love song
His flower   confidential. The Dalai Lama
His fields of old   Poison. The Sally Lama
His brutal children   Chanel tossed about!

—I'm the human violin   a short alarm. The sun ripped
Just erase   going to deliver more
Then, sandpaper   mistaken, eating sandy moray eels
I'm making a couch   erased from this earth,

Asia sleeps   nothing under my chin
Lechers riot   halving the hospital's hallways
Charging hair salons   mistaken among the willows
The wagon in   The Raja was good enough to

A folded doormat   ate the both of them in the car
Or my little car   er, parliament's been
German's laughing at your   feverish since Sunday
Some dabble in sewing or   or diligently configured!

CVII
The Solitary Drinker

One look from the woman galloping by
And my glasses fell off my nose. My wig turned white,
The moon got off the bus with a lemon pie, the lake trembled.
When she wants to take a bath, she leaves her shoes on

And the last thing she excuses herself to remove are her riding gloves.
George Washington kissed her once, mistaking her for a patriot named
          Madeline.
She was the granddaughter of a music teacher and she had a rosy complexion.
Everyone's babbling and crying out about the sunshine downtown and
          taking long naps in it.

No one's ever getting up from their spot. O bottomless cup
The billows of dark fog penetrate even
The saucer I set you down into.

Someone get me the waiter, or the bus boy with my check.
—I'll look over the taxes and everything I've eaten
And tear it apart, right beneath the trembling mouth of God!

CVIII
Leaving Days A Moon Mountain

Aren'tya whosis the space compadre whose plane did
Send morse code send aprons from send yer bride?
By all heavy or horses that won't be ridden, verily, di'nt
Poor Uncle Frederique help ya out vey back ven?

A comet or two angled at your chest but
One engine rocket with cable, placemats a long mellow endurance journey
Burned in the blue crystal of morning,
Swiftly arrived to save your Russian space station ass, loins and in-betweens!

All Molly and Me might appreciate is a ballsy once-around in the tail-fin of
        your car.
Do turbulences enrich your intellect?
In a parallel delirium

Am I my good sir you, each of us swimming in the others' coat?
Does we our furies forward each other our mail but not our collection of
        moon rocks?
Where is this paradise that we the pair of us deem it to dream of our
        mirrors and fire the ignitor rockets?

Fleurs du Mal

CIX
La Destruction

The sounds piling up in my shirt sleeves bother the demon in my bed.
He was swimming in this sea of words like an airplane too heavy for flight.
I received in the mail a taste for very hot mustard,
And it was implicit in the accompanying letter that the desire for more
          would never be torn out of me.

Sometimes love hides beneath the great skirts of Art
Taking the form of a sleeping blue woman,
And between her spread apart pretexts a cursing duck
Dresses my lever in a flaming post office.

The volts that run through my loins as I look upon the loins of the Lord:
Like taking Haldol and spilling hot tea on my pants. O million
Planes of the enemy, in favor of keeping dry words together

And throwing them in my eyes, full of confusion
From soldiers and their sweethearts, open green blessings
And the bloody clothes of La Destruction!

A Late Martyr
À Jo Ann Wasserman

Before even falcons at the top of the stairs sipping coffee
    Or maybe when I or I remember her hips her thighs
Okay, it can't be forgotten, her water table and her smoking jacket
    Dragging out behind her and the keys and someone is playing
        the piano.

In a flooded room or when I see an angel
    The air is doubtful and frequently
Your plane is circling almost out of fuel and a brown crocodile
    Is breathing heavily into my soup

The cabbie refuses to post his license. Instead he's cut out a snowflake
    And mounted it behind his ear.
One song rose red out of the radio, abbreviating
    Or cutting into the air conditioning. Presently

And I can't make out what he's saying. If this man
    And if we if he & I were chained together if we locked eyes
And if the traffic & the weather drown out the rest of him sadly
    I still bend over to see those young girls' underthings

Under the periodic table. At once you awoke from your coma and determined
    To paint the room again. Wide and well thought-out
An unsigned postcard my hairdresser blots out the sunrise
    Or with a glass of ginger ale a young Italian woman frowns and
        turns her gaze away.

All your luggage arrives on fire
    And the plane with no pilot lands on the bog.
Her ghost is strangled in splendor her scarf the whiskers
    Of leopards fit into the body of a tree.

* * *

Embarrassed by rose water the rooster or the door opens on gold in the
        bookie's office
    There's the paperweight as it should be
And stepping out with all the smokers and in his eye there's no secret to
        the flames:
    It's a diamond moving across the Dardanelles

One thing or the room is entirely empty
          Or is there room for a couch a chair or
All the eyes of the conspirators seek the sides of Everest
          And when the phone rings once they all respond with a brass band

Who's in the rain if not joyously or daring performers of fireball submission
          Of simply the fire kiss
Won't you couldn't you simply revoke the test scores of the angels
          And swim from here on their pleas to the petting zoo?

* * *

I suppose if what you're telling me is that she can't or she has a slow traipse
          There in the cupola the dome and her fingers are broken
That I stared at the backs of her thighs that on Tuesday I was in the pond
              with the ducks
          That she was with them or the queen of the komodo dragon

Her car has very few miles on it. Someone asked me before leaving me
          If it was her and if seven if she'd burned at the stake with a vampire
And no she was a senator. She walked in the exit door and might have torn
              her skirt only
          Sir I left to go shopping and for us forgot us

* * *

Only on the vine the cat allows and if you have never been able to buy
          your way into the game
          Oh there were for you grey geese my love, asleep or very
Or in the counting rooms they make a cake mix and though I lay my hair
              down on the runway asleep
          Leaving or as you walk down the staircase

The cab driver returns your call and your phone hums and a plane takes off
          one emergency lands
          Or are detectives will they strong-arm you forever
This month this mouth buys into every hand producing another cold tooth
          And Lassie rolls over and dies, finally

154

* * *

Before the crotch of the moon raiders before I was among the railroads or
       before the ducks were themselves devils
      Or before and before I broke into the tower in search of alchemy
And before we slept in peace or before we slept in peace and the doorbell
       rang out It was your
      Before the District Attorney's mysterious love affair with the tomb

Your epicurically nautical half-court game and the Tao of your three-point shot
      Crushed the wicked with an auto mechanic's grip
Otherwise the desert remained was already dry or no angels ever deserted you
      And constantly your constant jumpshot mostly rained down the most

CX (a)
The Both Of Them

Merely dangerous Latin Kings, bags of fat tomatoes,
The both of them or their bathhouses, long sofa-bed pull-out kisses or joyous
Cups of warm chocolate at sunrise, rising with the cockatoo in the window
    of an ice cream parlor. I throw a bit of my pastélé to a large bird
    but a small bird takes it away so I have to throw a bit more to the
    large bird who's still hanging around.
I was carving a drinking fountain out of an elephant's skull, but then one
    night I deserted the whole project and woke the next morning in a
    public park with my pants around my ankles and my ass exposed
    on the lawn.
Merely dangerous Latin Kings with bags of fat tomatoes, like a woman in a
    white T-shirt guarding her breasts in a surprising rainstorm

The both of them or their bathhouses echo with songs off dead sea-men's
    tongues, and although this park closes at midnight, the fountain
    isn't timed to stop until three.
The desert nomad's suitcase was thrown from the plane when it was
    discovered that he was really a desert nomad. Fortunately it landed
    on a beach, and eventually the sands pushed it back to him. The
    pastry chef forgot how to spell his name
And so started smashing a warm cranberry muffin onto sensitive
    documents for the stains it left like blood lifted from my aunt's
    wrists as she thrashed about indecisively in the tub. A glossy
    magazine ran an article about the wheat-only diet adopted by the
    soccer star
And ran photographs of orange growers rioting outside his hidden fortress
    after he'd reneged on a promotional contact. He ran onto the field
    at the start of his last game with a hand-painted banner that read
    "They're poisoning the fruit!"
The both of them or their bathhouses echo in the night the lapping tongues
    of mermen after leaping into the lap of the book store cashier!

The both of them, pinching the Pyrennees after borrowing a nickel,
    climbing over the lip of a crescent moon, dressing up like the
    Michelin Tire man only to break down crying
From the pinches of milkmaids leaping out from behind the soup tureen!
    Like a small dog you never stop barking at nothing. The sound of
    your own voice
Finds its only equal in the sound of a rolled-up newspaper swinging at your
    nose and missing. The stars in the bathhouse ceiling shine down
    on you

And Venus drops a chocolate sweeter than Sappho singing "Jailhouse Rock"
On the both of them, and damned if the Pyrennees don't pinch you
        through your riding pants where the sun don't shine.

The both of them tear down the curtain during the half-time show and call
        out the names of women they wish they'd never slept with
Whose body funks still rattle in their closets. Crates of stolen tea arrive on
        the shores of the island
The girls had their yearbook photo taken on, their bodies twined with
        octopuses.
Careless laissez-faire economics applied to the murders of the MacNeil-
        Lehrer News Hour,
The both of them, smoking their torn-apart prom dresses and lifting up the
        hems to reveal eleven kangaroos they'd been hiding beneath. Latin
Kings, where are you now? I invoke your presence in this poem in blue and
        orange basketball shorts knowing that if you'd seen her as I'd seen
        her you'd want to try to do what I wanted to try to do in the
        boys' bathroom of a nearby high school, but the door was open
        onto the hall and I was afraid someone would see. Perhaps you'd
        do it anyway. Perhaps you'd do it out in the hall.

At last the view from inside the whale shows up on a tour of the Plankton
        Museum, and the front man for the tour forces a fifteenth cough
        drop into his cake hole and mutters something about Mina Loy
        and how she appeared to him in a dream, on a staircase in a nightie
With two tires and a really oversized King James Bible signed by King
        James himself. An overweight leg-breaker—freelancing these days,
        but working mostly with a team of guitar-wielding bruisers
Named, respectively: René, The King of the Gumdrops, Billy the Law
        Maker, and Saint Theresa—
Was eating refined sugar from a bag all weekend wearing nothing but a
        dinner jacket,
And that was the last I saw of him, at the Plankton Museum, leaning against
        the fence that blocked off the staircase to Mina Loy's bedroom.

Two giant tires had taken on the roles in a local play of the White Rabbit
        and the March Hare
But one had gotten a flat in a local bakery and was prescribed a long rest
        at some sea-side spa where packs of wild and ambitious dogs roam
        at night
Dressed in loin cloths stolen from radials & sun gods at the height of the
        day turning smiles and laughter to sour grimaces.
Talk amongst yourselves about nothing in particular for a moment while I
        decide if I'm going to finish this poem, or leave on a small boat
        bound for the Sahara to see a

Pair of tires about a fat senator's pardon for the crime of being late to his
       race horse's cocktail party!

After all, who throws dice at an ostrich? The both of them, having been
       their own judge for years
And throwing out the entire front wall of their house so we could witness the
       work involved in Balinese pail dancing on the Road Less Traveled
In which Sisi balances a door knob weighing more than Noah's flood
On her forearms while her mother runs her fingers through her russet tresses?
Which of you, having never thrown dice at an ostrich is really suited to be
       their judge?

Especially when it is our responsibility to bring Lois Lane to justice for all
       the insinuations she managed to make in the deli in just
One day, Friday, while Jules Verne drank his liquor with his sled dogs and
       lime, and the hanging judge painted landscapes of three chapels,
And your religion got voted in as the one with as many pauses as Quaker
       Oats in a hurricane,
And Tanya Harding laughed and laughed because the law enforcement
       agencies were all responding to the 911 call of a sea lion
Rocking on its belly in a canoe on the violent river that flows past
       the hydroelectric plant that provides the juice for all the lime
       juicing machines.

In a car the both of them reached between their toes searching for a matchbook
       with the name of my favorite steak and roller derby house.
They poured a decanter of wine on the sidewalk through the open window
       and before forcing the singer out of the car in the rain, they
       floored it and lit the secret supply of nitro so that flames shot from
       the tailpipe, and they rocked on towards the highway on the verge
       of breaking the sound barrier
And just as I was fussing with my photograph of Desi Arnez in his infancy,
       haunted by the approach of a dark phantom in the form of
       administrative offices
That rifles through his handkerchief drawer battling with giants armed with
       socks filled with yardsticks
The car—between the two of them they couldn't find their own mother in
       a coffee house filled with Swazilanders.

The deputy cried to the Lord "All I want is to write one sonnet worth my
       weight in millet and to locate
The comma you've hidden in 'Sentimental Journey,' and sure enough,
       from its steel perch, a condor made rich

By a nationally televised quiz show threw down nuts and bricks made of
    tartar sauce left out to dry since Watergate,
And I still maintain that their shapes bore the face of the Cowardly Lion
    blasted into them by a laser beam powered by the sun,
Although the deputy prays over his meals "Lord, all I want is to write one
    sonnet that will fling open the doors to the local peep show

So I can see if my mother is involved in a dull conversation with a
    gentleman and his muffin,
And permit me to sing my prayers low enough to shy that condor back to
    his cave."
One night I was dining with a sting ray in an Italian restaurant whose poems
    about the both of them he was trying to trade me for my car keys
When like a magic trick, who should appear in the kitchen door but
    Sappho, keeping our waiter with the tea service
From telling us if the sea was involved in a dull conversation with a
    gentleman and his muffin!

But you can only *delay* the mail, Sappho! The multitudes of letters that
    pass through the sickening hands of the post office
Are greater than the pails full of semen contained in the belly of Venus on
    the morning after the night before the fleet ships out!
Mina Loy was dancing on the deck of a ship with reindeer beside her in the
    night as pool sharks and transient extra-terrestrials waved machetes
Around in circles above their heads tracing in the firmament the words
    spoken by a pair of dueling
Mailmen. Sappho is climbing the steps to the post office.

More bells than Venus had said could rescue us from our surly mandates
Were singing and swimming through the libraries caroling, disguised as
    naiads just birthed from the mouth of Summer
In polyester hospital gowns. We descended disguised as the Loch Ness
    Monster in his youth in search of our bed linens.
The grumpy ocean dropped below our feet enchanted
By the many bells hanging around the necks of All-Star baseball pitchers
    and race car drivers!

Sappho, more than twice a day, had been coming down to bang on the
    locked door of my blast furnace,
When she caught in her rabbit trap an ailing colt. She whisked him away to
    her parlor for tea.
She fitted him for the saddle of a mounted archer in the pasture of a soup
    cook in the afternoon, and in the evening she took him to strip
    clubs where

John Donne sat beating off while a golden man whipped him with his
        limp dick to pay for his supper
Of enough celery stalks to block the doorway of my blast furnace.

They say the deputy is trying to sell the both of them his menthol cigarettes
And the mail is piling up lazily in the home of the justice of the peace
        where he cuts gaping holes in his poems to the moon
And sends them hot across the wires each night to the duke of the
        underworld and the tennis court judges
Who steal off towards the railroad stations and leap forth from giant
        pastries at the riverbank!
And the deputy is trying to sell the both of them his menthol cigarettes!

Femmes Damneex
Delphine et Hippolyte

i.

By the pale white wine and the lamp light that was lying there,
On the depth of her foul mouth, pregnant with the smells of a circus tent,
A cross-gendered hippopotamus woke up mid-way through an attempted
      pocket picking.
Who was lifting the keys to her ride home? None other than November's
      Candy Striper of the Month.

She was digging above the sound of an oil painting of a blast furnace
In her navel for yesterday's bottle of sun tan lotion
Which her midget aunt had loaned to her after stealing it from a wayward
      sailor whose neck she snapped when he turned to look at her ass.
He'll never wonder again if the point where the sky meets the ocean as the
      morning passes over them is more blue or more green,

His eyes are closed like a box of Valentine's chocolates that falls from your
      paramour's arms in a car accident.
In the hedgehog's lair the dull assistant to this morning's shapely (but
      mad) scientist,
In whose breasts blood rushes as in the veins of the army preparing
To serve her, crosses a picket line of suffragettes though they'd helped tie
      her boat to the dock.

Listening to the sound of her feet, but calm as when flying on an aeroplane
      staffed by dishwashers,
The farmer's wife's beautiful seamstress opens up a lake in her lover's eyes
In front of the tower guards of the animal fortress who look her over and pray
They'll graduate from cooking school with their degrees and having seen
      her name written out in gigantic letters on the side of a ship so
      they might learn to open doors with their teeth.

Beautiful fort that makes us feel our age, that boils water for tea with no frills,
Super dictionary-class alphabet soup diners, she steams towards now you in
      a plane broken free from an amusement park ride
Leaving behind her the designs she'd made on yawning beneath an elm
      tree, and she is sallying towards you
To reclaim and unmake all the tender mercies due a pocket billiards
      champion in Kampuchea.

She is looking into the eye of the tempest at a pail whose cold time did not
      come to wash away off the beach.
The singer choked on the song he'd found in the trauma ward,
The Desert God studied the contents of his pockets but there was no end
To the line of bus boys who hoped to make the tip here that would clear
      their names in the kitchen.

Hippo-lite, dogstar to the stars, what do you think of these things when
      your chores are done?
Do you stand next to the trash compactor with the superintendent
      crushing the knees of your enemies until they offer to walk away
With the best of your roses sold off at bargain rates while you stroll out
      into the sunlight in a sack dress with no reason and no job to call
      your own
While the wind shuffles and pours porridge and flees from the crime scene?

My kisses land on the legs of round-faced women who glance at me only
      briefly with the eye of a passing elephant caravan
Where dyke masseurs shrink back from the oceans our fore-fathers crossed
And each of the Grand Tetons pauses to gun its motor at a stoplight and
      see if anyone slips in on their passenger side
Like a breakfast cereal delivery truck driver who finds he's unwittingly
      swapped stockings with his father's sister

As they passed one another outside the boiler room. What did you have to
      say then? As lords strapped L's to their chests to signify their
      leaping free of the shackles of age,
As horses and jewelers took off their shoes before the hot beach sands...
Hippolyta, meditating on the coast, turn this mallet over in your hands.
      Examine it
In the shower. Toil, and lift your hatchet to throw it at me. Climb onto my
      back. Mount me like a dog giving me motion sickness.

Turn towards me with a yellow plate in front of you, howling for
      hypnotists to spring to life and give up their concentrated stares,
      eating instead all
The porridge undulating beneath your gaze and your charms and all the
      times you said "bombs away" instead of "good-bye."
Lady Day will not sing of you or apologize for passing you on the stairs. I
      lift up the headset of the telephone and a voice volleys across
And I go to sleep next to you while the projectionist changes reels.

In May you are polite as a beatnik and lift out of your yellow fever:
"I am not standing behind a grate on this point and after that first mistake
      no one's ever tried to fence me in again.

Mad at elephants, I shuffled and was juicily inky-eyed,
But anyone who came after me got knocked around by my eight terrible
wheat-eating commandantes singing.

I can feel the hospital workers mining into my shoulder blades for
movable tracts
And for black armies that arrive at night to drink sodas with the skeletons
they've been paired with
Whose house keys press their lips against car doors begging to be driven
down those roads where the wind is a breath
That slams down on us at the end of the day like a car door, crushing all
our fingers, and parting our hair like a farm boy's.

Have we earned our commission by committing strange acts with pack animals?
Tell me, poor mouth, of the troubadours that have climbed your stairs for
your efforts.
I shiver all over in the rain when in your sickness you cry out to me,
'My Angel!'
And my pen leaks a bloody stain through my jeans pocket and my mouth
tries to find you among greenery in an alleyway.

But don't look at me when I've had too much coffee. My cock thinks only
of you
In a public toilet crushing gems with your bootheels as your sister enters
Parliament
And you both are wearing the same dress in my mouth
And the cat calls go down into rivers wrapped in chains to map the depths
of our diction!"

The barn-door closer shook out a coconut from her second-hand crinolines,
And like a wall that had been painted over three times and on the third
pass is covered in a foot thick coat of iron
A poison air came back with a still drier foot, singing and banging its pot,
if only to say
"What's up doc? Are we going to lift love off its feet to see how many
ostrich eggs it's got hidden in its nest or sit dully in the parlor and
talk about hell all evening?

Your fine sour taste was brought to me by the newsboy from Quebec, and
since I can't ever return you for my 5¢
I'll open up the furnace door to melt you down and send you back to
Parliament, and dance around, a simpleton
Solving problems by driving up their middles when no other solution
announces itself or shows its promotional film clip.

Among other things the barn door swinger has mixed up above her head
   are truth, yellow jackets and Springtime!

Certainly residents of Southern Fla. would like to dance with me. The
   same step maybe not, but certainly under the same spell! Right out
   onto the driveways in front of their homes and onto the roadways
   of Rte. 1,
Cuban immigrants and their chauffeurs, into the night at their leisure,
And none of the chauffeurs are crushing gemstones with their uniforms or
   burying them under the bodies of trees
Or forcing them into the sun, the only hiding place left for love's solitary
   accountants.

Go then, if that's your game! Look for a co-op board
Who'll send you to school in a small sea front town where you'll have to
   live in a basement
And eat only the dull remains of the headmistress's dinner of liver and beans.
You can get back to me later on how many scars you've received from the
   bit and being lashed by her reins...

If only you'd been able to content yourself taking cold baths and living the
   life of a waitress!"
Several deer on May's lawn, cooking up griddle cakes with their sleeves
   rolled up while a large cloud shaped like the epileptic president
   rolls overhead
& bursts suddenly cry "We haven't got the money or enough
   understanding of the monetary system to have this conversation
   before sunrise,
But a giant with a large butt, the same giant that ate my dog,

Is getting paid to cook recipes discovered in the 'Suggestions' box!
No one raised this monster up to jam his mitts
Into the Sun God's fresh cream, which is to say nothing of changing the
   lightbulb at the back of the Frigidaire!
This is the same giant who set fire to his own hand and stood there letting
   it broil until his blood sang out

And he came riding out onto our farm insisting that he'd lost his way in
   the world
And that only by studying our dog could he be sure to find his way home again.
I'd like to see him thrown into the pit where man-eating insects are
   recruited for wages
And pour fresh cream over the boulder that seals his tomb!"

ii.

—Go down go down lawn chairs and tables! Shoplift the minutes we've set
        aside for canasta
Go down with the chemistry set of pesticides' timetable!
Plunge into an open Bible in a Jehovah's Witness' lap, where all B movies
Run their titles across the marquis and paper the walls of their homes with
        patterns of musical instruments letting the wind blow through the
        empty string on their flagpoles.

Make bouillabaisse, mixing in an orange-scented cologne with your
        soccer cleats.
Brown fools, bitten on the ass by the dog of your desires,
Never will you pour your rage out of a soup tureen
And the song that rings on in your head will broadcast over every channel
        on Japanese Television.

Never will a cold silk stocking be pulled cleanly out of your orifices
And every golf ball you club off of your tee will fall into a bog with a sigh.
        A sickly miasma will overtake you at the wall every day as five
        o'clock rings out, and you will be too old and it will be too late to
        pick up your prescription.
Fill a trout's apartment with the other inflatable life rafts which lantern
        carrying pool sharks overlooked
Although the smell of the shipwreck worked its way into their bodies
        long afterwards.

May a housecleaning ape with no dick devote his daily efforts to raise the
        dead to you
And raise the hem of your dinner jacket and twist your hair into a spacious
        home for vermin
And answer the door when furious winds blow bondsmen in to collect
        your husband from your wedding bed for jumping bail after
        revealing government science secrets in the Cub Room, too drunk
        to realize
He'd broken your chair and left you lying on your back like a painter fallen
        outside of her drop cloth.

Your loins will produce only purple children, errand boys with palsied
        knees and condemned buildings
That atrophy and fall in hunks into your beehive as you stroll the emptied
        lanes done up to look like a wolf in curlers.
Cast your vote for fate to leave you standing if you like, discord has already
        given the word for dirty hands to be sent up to your hotel room
And finish pulling you out of your suitcase where you've been hiding!

CXI
Femmes Damnées

The beast paused over his desk
Turning the wheel
Slapped again
Twelve cold loves

After the moon's spirit broke
Jazzed by the bouquets
Shouldered or butted hard
In the woods. A woodsman

Leaving behind his sister's grave. Leaving from
A stone cross. A wide bellied ghost.
Cut open
Seven nuns at the train station

At least the east
In Parliament his aunt crosses the floor
Calling out the names hurled
Asleep at the dinner table.

The gorgon ate
Remembered a fountain
Two cookies battled over
The fire alarm. The spume of gassy

No rocks or monsters no demons
Taking tickets
Church mice in the town hall
Christ falling off the wagon too

You are a porpoise.
Sisters. I love like my aunt
Dollars and asparagus
Sure are full. Focusing

CXI
Femmes Damnées

Come on, a beetle? Do you think   on the couch her mint
She turns their eyes   touching the edge of the sea
And leers fall looking for footholds   seeing hands approaching
On the deuces that linger   the language teacher standing before the icebox

The ones, hearts pried   the confessional tipped over
In the fondue pot   his Russian Pontiff's hat jarred
Going for the shoulder plates   onto his cranium. The endive tipped the fence
And cruising in the green woods   a young garden

Others, your sister walks in   walking between beans and graves
Crossing the rocks   whole ghosts
Where St. Antoine turned up the volume   cut open a bar of soap passing
The signs were freshly painted and   music come forward seven songs

Getting sick over the starboard rail   violins, oboes, fried dough
Who was dancing softly on the cross   our old country kitchen
Apparently, you can tap dance on seconal   tumbles down the hill a fiery look
O venture capitalists, enormous door   from an old dead phonograph

And Gene Autry's dog. Don't look at its face   loves of scabbard-wielders.
       His home
Who, recalling how the faucet   a long dress to the ankle
Battled in the darkened woods   at eight o'clock I eat a cookie alone
E'cu-me? Who been sittin' in my seat?   alarum ringing as the queen is taken

Over the register. Ode to her mons.   a ghoul with his mouth open in the
       supermarket parking lot
Dead lorry driver. Grrr   a ghost at the check out
Church cherishers. Dan finally   next one goes out to my club-footed lover
All-over tan. Decreed plainly   if you have two feet I'll cry & drown

You who cast your vote for drug-law reform   the ass goes down smoothly
Skin-chafers, I   autumn I head for the plains
For your death threats at dawn   your flowers are out of the can
And the urinals damn our   your bankers can't read a map

Lady Bouncers

Lady Brioche ate herself to death   are sure-shot accountants
Producing a set of candle holders   eat the sister's clean shoes
But wasn't it the end of all days   on the edge. Bullets strung across
      their bosoms
Under Lady Nell's labia   had never witnessed childbirth

O poet anesthesiologist, in my   in my family
Favorite arboretum a lawn chair   judge of the sandbox, never paying rent
Tumbles and a wolf in hiking shorts   one month's rent among char-
      broiled millions
Unlit, culling Laramie's uncertain   Nah. I jam frequently

Ate the bear, ate all the bedsheets   blah blah blah. A lightning bug reads
      a little magazine
We offered a tour of the towers   like two bouncers on
Detained by the arid sweatshop and   Daffy Duck's soft red lips.

Wand. Ventricle. Man-eating   day. Is the bullshit on Oprah broadcast
      round the world?
O Mort, con artist on the verge of becoming too   Sorry, the mountain's
      closed. On a tray
On the myrtles, insects   tea, the black cypresses, the president?

Laughing Tundra Song

Some sick men bend car parts to cool the influence
Antique urns have at parties. Beat out your joy gone from gloves
Into a fine sandwich. Yankee assholes, you can't mow the lawn if you don't
       pick up your trash.
The first method was to bless the child under a veil never having seen it.

The fire department screams down the street as I jump away from my ideas,
Up the entrance they run on company time, a chick pokes through its shell
       and that's it.
Try to get off the train and they'll beat you until you're hungry again;
You think you could live on this anger, but will it fill your stomach?

Jade goddess drove the van all day to Washington.
Her arrival was pure as new underwear, the jeweler locked her up crying.
Blue clarinets prove her folk-loric history in the rain, though infrequently.

"Who blames her, the poor old wench I remember."
—A postcard from a monkey after the death, add it to the pile.
In years her cruel feet dancing will be done like a vapor.

CXIV
In The Stocking Factory

The woman rings the bell coherently *(Sadie's burned herself badly)*
Training her horse *(I lost my keys in the bushes)*
Love's poisons. Three feet *(Legs lift out of the morning)*
Gliding on the sidewalk, some mice *(All of her skin)*
Take a cracker from a junkie. *(She loves a man in the bush)*
Greeting and smiting with a halberd *(Sea monsters now offer their hands,*
       who always at first)
Young construction workers kneel *(In these hallowed drain pipes)*
Before the king's hard body. *(Doo-wopped for lariats)*
She walks all over the dressers. *(And leans on the sultan's pillows)*
She dances in the plaster. *(Laughing at my home-made townhouse)*
An apple yells out louder than the finish line. *(THE DESI ARNEZ*
       CHAIN LETTER)
She crouches. She adjusts her gait on the window's ledge. *(Infrequently, on)*
The world has wandered in to the supermarket. *(A cat-caller and a nay-sayer)*
A Mafia don stands behind his cement mixer *(Taking the easter bow tie to court)*
Brushing spiderwebs carefully from his hair. *(Whose entire Detroit family)*
She ignores the lawn chair. *(There goes another lost plumber)*
On the verandah, night *(And when the time comes to walk into the darkness)*
Looks out of the face *(on the day the lamb, or)*
Of the newly born. *(I see something coming, aces and electric eels)*

CXV
La Béatrice

Interviewing these, the desert of the cinders or the grassless plains
And if I came out with a platter or, in layman's terms,
And if then, penniless, on guard for greater evils
I tried to augment and the dairy farm was soon and slowly so close to the
   point of my sword
And you were envisioning we envisioned if at the mid-point in our lives we
   descended down a well
Only the mirage was of flames of coastal workers and roller coasters and a
   large storm fell on you
Whose only identification was flattened in a hat band and bit by devils
Would it seem to you that some breads were insensitive and others
   merely curious?
Are you many considerations coldly hosing down the mirage?
And, like the barefoot peasants you feathered on the road,
I lean unflinchingly or laughter at the butcher shop falls between us
In exchange for one hand blocking out the road signs and one hand
   covering your eyes.

Think what do you have to lose you were thrown from the carriage
Think of it here, in this jacket the brown city bends over you
And the lake the catalogues of wind-swept hair
Isn't it this and your steps inside the pie plate already you must sleep on
   the bomb, with the bomb
The gumshoe, and he said the historian leaves vacancies his bedroll
And because he knows how to jump and play, how to roll out the
   cement mixer
He would sing a hairdresser's duller days
Into the corners. The steak cooking on the hood of your car, the
   underwater ruins and flowers
And we aren't we the same, the authors of these old bricks rubbing
   together in the walls
And speaking aloud and hurling glass at the crowd in three parades
   throughout the city?

I will have already been sick (my organization is also as high as the
   mountains
And do I mind that her, her nudity her naked body blots out the devils the
   mountains for days)
And don't you turn your head as you simply drive off the road or are you
   simply under the bank the vault
With no alibi? I saw you inspecting the animal handlers and their leashes

And who what burglars haven't canceled checks and locked themselves in
        the bathroom?
Queen of my heart whose face divides the highway
Who laughs up dirt into my hair when I lift my heart
And you they sing often of your godliness your amphibious car.

Les Met Alphonse, Hortense And Pamplemousse In My Accountant's Office With A Vampire

This woman
pen in hand sky-
colored from Asian an
Hippopotamus not her not
a sneezing giraffe
not at the end of
the walkway
rain soaked hat
licorice quinine winding
around the chef's
soup ladle around
the hot
lamps a snake
or sour plums Most
importantly
God looks out
an open window a sour
plum Spain
in flames
on the school bus tied
to a tree looking out
the eye piece stopping
in the road to
eat a cupcake Carry
a cupcake around
over your head
champion the ringleader
the bullfighter Mexico
Grubber I can't even
spell your filthy name
the name a cow sings
A hurler or 3X
the humidity and up
and dies on us
in the aisle
at the awards ceremony
The chemist
a vowel a nosegay in his
buttonhole He and I
we liked

to see the sparks
before the rocket
backfired flames
melting even our
nametags eyebrows
It didn't bother us
So the Earl of Sandwich
his fingers a small
seamstress at night
a worn down
and sour plum spacing
as God looks dreamily
through the window
and full Police cars
or screaming and Israel
diseased hugging close
disaffected elephants
sniffing Bills flutter
in the fireplace or the singer
lined up to hear me sing
A baby crying or in a desert
an end to villainy
The lunge Leslie
Albert
on the cliff nothing useful
but Joe begins litigation
as the moon
wakes up happy knows
Or a bank manager or
stock broker lists the
books settles
cures and I'm stuffing
a pig with
sunlight on the porch
In the light
reading
the kitchen inventory
At least until the sutures
the sultan I'm walking
out of the gas
station
as the rats smash bottles
against the moon
Thimbles in equations wait
their turn stop

and all my electronic
football shuts down in silence
A dead fly
In both their hair
Damn these fury
angels whose checkbooks
wage ineffectively
as vowels
as Ma Rainey the queen
embark
Hawaii

What else squarely
studying where paradise
is on my shoes and
lights up certainly
bad guy a hulkish
one limping
and sideways Stretching
a walk like a day-long
nap out The cheese
plate flying all I have
are yogurts raisins a twist
in the road and she
My airplane sings its
brand identity draws
out the lawyer
eats most of my breath
but our airline flying
in the blood
in the red and iron
But which is the gay bar
or the saturnian rings
where a sauntering bristle shirt
pregnant or already given birth
feminists look up
out of cars or the desert
where white blood cells
My accountant's office
a Jewish man with no legs
only a fish tail
and he showed me
the way
Ten or so decibels
ten vacuum cleaners

you see South America's
pack animals
and so fraülein a bathtub
disproves all my banknotes
at Madame Coot's Who
lied about the dodo
The mannequin in a
pissing contest with an ant
while the payoff came in
by bird traffic
or iron ore in pigs
have you farted
I created
a television for the blind
my blood singing going down
tumbling a fat lip trembling
confusion like a fire drill
the deer the antlers the buck
where the fence collapsed or
next week the Queen
taxes thieves or communism
The President already took
down the gauntlet
wax wings and in the desert
the plasterer has dust in his eye
Leaves the desert signs on
with the merchant marines
as the boat
the desert
Where Pythagoras meets Bermuda
currency is not available
I lean my shoulder
to tip the boat to Spain
and anyway wind
or pendulum
and are we less together
as divers

CXVI
Un Voyage À Cythère
No Seats On The Plane

Monsignor brought a bird   birds lit up by all cookbooks
And phoned liberally   the entourage spending days braiding
The navy's annual pig roll   under a ceiling with no nude paintings
In walked an angel in real V   rays of a dead star wrapped around

What is this island twisted   sad and black? It's what there is to see
We continued to talk, ignoring the check   we are famed for our few
        Chinese sons
The Spanish movie with no sound or teeth   too uneducated in the old
        gardening songs
Listen to me, apple danish   it's a poor potato.

Island of twelve egrets and   eating with her feet like a dog!
Dylan Thomas' tiki Venus   Leisure class. She writes admiringly
Order now! Detain the sea   flat as his cologne,
And charge the spirits by the hour   damn our Red Cross lawn furniture

Ringing island with all colors but green   green, plain. Flowers close
Famed for ancient jams   on golf courses across the nation
Where herds of label-wielding dogs   cursing his admiration
Roll out their own incense chortling   sends her an empty garden above
        sea level

Where the cement mixers chill   turning the ram's horn!
—See, there never was more than   her rabbit ran in terror from the
        pilgrim's wig
A deserted roll call where birds   troubled by her eager, grey shouts
I travel between my aunt's bar   one thing by itself!

It never was a temple   to the brown grocery store
Where the president made her entrance in a yellow   lovers of snowfall
Everyone's already filled their bellies on flan   writing a name on the
        challenger's chariot
In between the ballet and the dressing room   stealing the breeze from
        the airlines' passengers

But the queen left her reason in a vase   held him against the coat of the
        easy president
Pouring trouble for birds   with our letter-sized white vases
We roped the Connecticut Senator in his jeans   there was a martini
        resting on three of the branches
But Sheila left the room   in black, like a cypress.

The Pope's biting swans   at home in the pasture
Never entrusted with rations   screaming. A clock already against the wall
Each one a banana, bringing   like the gas man, his nose poisoned by
In each coin purse, blood   knowing the difference between bread and
        soup bread.

The city of eyes dropped   trout, and the adventure to the foundry
The intestines weighed   him cooling on top of the cutlasses
Eating with a broom handle, the gorgeous   gorging on hideous delicacies
A wolf takes me up in his cessna   noses absolutely enchanted.

Underneath the racks of pants   a troupe of water jumpers or four footed
The museum reopened as a school   tower-gnawers and Rodan
A bigger, riskier wager   beaten. One million's agitating
In comes my former manicurist   interred with your help.

My aunt used to always say "see there"   child of a Chelsea bathroom
Silently cutting up my amusement   suffering the insults
An expiration date   cattle prod cult.
And the peaches that fell   You have interrupted the ton boy.

Foolish watch maker, your dollars   dealers are the small miners!
I smell. I'll inspect the Pope's   detained members afloat
In comes Miss Never-Took-A-Sick-Day   climbing once again, the stairs
        to my dentist's office
The long defiled flower   feel my dentures growing old.

Before you, skinny devil   bedeviling the memories of pop-stars in the
        Maritimes
I mailed myself toes and beaks   ate out the sewing machines, the chair
From car and boat vandals   ants and black panthers
Who have grown bored with my aunt Amy   don't atrophy in my chair. Three

The ceiling in the state's char house   the cripples came together
Woe is me! You were the night   black and singing, a small voice leaving
        me behind
Lads! I ate the javelin! In comes   as in an epic novel set in the Suez canal
The seven-veiled dog   a little dance, a little leg, a little blood.

In your heavy island oven-users!   I have never found the boat
One gimlet puts me back a week   Where my picture is swinging...
—Ah Monsignor! I am your donor   more discoveries break down and
        eat licorice
Stop thinking about my dog   early, my division sends you chocolates!

L'Amour Et Le Crane

Lamplight gov'nor each assisting the crane
       From opening the sidewalk café, granulated
And or sandy on Sunday how many, your brass leaps from the train
       When confronted with a doggish smile.

So if lesbians in the wind or on line at the bank buy you a round, pushy
       Who climbs the taxi cab window shuts on your hand, the cave
Mouth sings, Shelby come again, mount my leg, billiards leave me with
         lemons only
       But I'm mostly more fond of ether, air

A globe lit up from within by a refrigerator bulb
       Takes me to the gas station, a classroom, the ether
Has me cradled in its arm when the car hits the lamppost at sixty I am his
         only love I am in the grille
       Like a soup ladle a song of ore.

I'm listening. The crane bounces checks intentionally gov'nor
       But before the jaws of life come out I request my own broken
         space station
A seizure, the iron operator yelling into the yarn ball
       When will he be finished with it, the quota, the moon

Buggy again bumps up to your mouth below sea level. Is she a believer
       In the swordfish, the pill? Each one through enemy airspace
My strategy as it stands is to sell parts of my car-crash brain
       Each motion sickness eating me out in my chair

RÉVOLTE

CXVIII
The Widow Of Saint Pierre

What is it that do you make of this, floating by on antihistamines
While the monthly the tools and we these green days you get up out of
    your chair to go out and see a film.
With a tire iron George went and with him the wind
His checkbook blew open all the soft or brittle notes his affairs afire in the
    blast furnace.

These, those who sing for blood who sing for a flotilla of secretaries and
    more tire irons
A song the song they sing it seems to me the wind enters, comes between
    us to wash our feet our mouths
Doesn't it? Then what, or bad or grey or I went to bed straight from the
    fields singing let me have their voluptuous coffin
Let the movie be of me with my arms raised above my head in a vineyard
    and sassy

Sassing the mouth of Jesus O don't you remember the jeering the life or
    the dinner
In your simple house, a small city, you broke into my hands a chocolate
    cookie with almonds
It's all on the film! Who's into the city where rats bruise the clouds our
    mouths close around bruises
And if only then the ignobles the ministers rode in on the backs of mules
    with plantains in their laps and their wives seated behind.

Was it him then? Did the bank open and the wind enter on tip toe
To throw the dice in the vault with the bank guards and the day's lunch
    sighing in the deposit boxes
And was it him? Do you still feel his grip on your shoulder?
In the back of your brain or where else a great fog rising from the humidor

Or when your body and when the ocean the tide comes in, one pleasant
    fisherman's body landed with a thud in the fields

And an orange ruffy, with his fins pulled off only if then he was swimming
        in his blood and not yet a song
In the sewer, pouring out of the front of the Do you remember me? In
        these pants
When you were merely just an introduction to chinese food and before you
        stood in the store window modeling Bible scenes

Were you ever did you ever raise up the blinds on a bright morning and
        see a boat
Or two separate winds filling their pockets or then she turned aside to
        clean up after the birds.
Where did the two of them fall down at the end of the day? A mountain?
        Surely one soft year ago on the train
These for days passing factories and you bounced me on your knee while
        flowers and her vast concern the water

Where liquored up and gone flying a cessna is it easy to keep track of your
        own luggage?
Do both the winds do you forget all the villains the marching brass bands
Or are you the master of chinese food at last? The mortician the
        reincarnator hasn't he
Or did you never write the papers never print of the flap before the fog the
        ocean your elegant romance?

Certainly you know for sure that I sort the mail. When I wish, I mail you a fish
And that's when the world ends or isn't milk a part of the sister of your dreams?
My promise I will use all the gloves you leave in my closets and perish by
        leaving your gloves!
There isn't a pair of rocks kneeling or do we understand one another? I'll
        have he has when will it be finished?

Abel And Cain

i.

I run ably to the door of the wood eating ate
God a tiny smile a long, long sofa. I ate God a long long sofa he sat sitting small

I run to a field a collapsed grain silo the fangs
Of the trains heading up the ramp and blurred me I held all my small
       wheats to my breast

I run ably babbling your you a bag of you is enough
You push your nose flat against an aquarium window shoe store windows

I run cussing within, your policeman's banquet a pair of handcuffs
Has the oxen ever met his end thrown overboard over the side of a boat?

I run to answer the door. Your entrails
Hurled at me from a dairy farmer's truck just as his wife runs home
       cooking an old chicken in a pot

I run to answer "all in" you see me and raise me you see me to the end of
       my sentence a Louis Malle novel
And every detailed boat follows behind the shutters to the beginning.

I run to where the door is. The bell is huffing hot before the window
In your foyer. Daddy's home. He calculates

I run in come in in. Downtown and the outdoors
Trouble in the frost, defrost, pay for a chalk horse each horse only an outline

I run at a bell at a beauty or loving corpuscle, a pullman porter
Falls fainting outside. The days are small.

I run if you can the dog on the bed rolling over in muck in rude
Potato skins the gardener's at a game of aces and small estates.

I run now if you are able you believe your bedside crumbles at the hands
       of brutes and highwaymen
Bring down the munitions of old boy's forest!

I run to get in on only under the road
The train and his family were cutting a boy's woods.

ii.

Ah! I was running ably until you charged me with an iron lung train
Grasslands overtook all of me while the sun just smoked!
What were you running into? Your suitcase a kiss
Isn't enough a soufflé a smothering sandwich.
I was running ably. Here's the whole true story:
The ferry is capsized by the polecat!
I was running can't I up onto the mountain the ceiling
And there on the terrace God stuck out his foot.

Les Litanies De Satan

For The Fork

Hoboes working in train yards on oboes bust a lip or what does she make
      change with fire tongs
So you transitory or transporting the sort of private change making lounges

    O Satan, lemme get two slices

Open prints or once I was confined to a Dairy Queen where the supreme
      court justices hung out
Aching for Vancouver's everyday tea-time dress codes but before one
      could flatulate

    O Satan, one to go and five zeppoles

You unlocked the hoboes toiling on cheap-skate trombones. The supermarket
      has an underground cheese showroom
The warrior the supervisor and his family sleeps on folding cots angry or
      birdlike the moisture

    O Satan, square and a slice to go please

On the mid-sections of slaving hoboes whose leprous or somewhere, there,
      pastry chefs prepare a cake for their jailed accountant
And in the frosting write "with love." The government puts to sleep some
      heavenly dice throwers

    O Satan, how much are those babies

Hoboes slavering away in a vestibule already singing death your wheelchair
      half-eaten or a herd of sea cows
Giving birth to invisibility. This autumn I squeeze

    O Satan, can I have a cup of water

The locksmith's cheeks and prescribe or my credit card flattens out the sea
      at eight o'clock leaving
The key beneath the door knocker and your travelogue unbelievably crowds
      into a doorway to escape the cold

    O Satan, can I get a slice, two slices actually, fresh tomatoes pepperoni

The key doesn't work angels or the storm is finally calming your change
purse spills onto the sidewalk in full view of those
Ladies whose jalopy extends past the cashier's office to the jeweler's down
the block. He uses

O Satan, can I get a slice not too hot please?

Blind men laboring clearly You know them, recognize them? The long racks
of bombs and missiles
Or don't you and so severely let people know at the day's end the cool metals

O Satan, spinach roll and a fresh mozzarella

The locksmith alchemizes. A soupless metropolis has no views, also
no waterfowl
Only sheeps attired in flame retardant wool frocks lately designed for horses

O Satan, lemme get a baby to go

The locksmith, consoling a man who has dropped his failed asparagus
soufflé at his feet
We applaud your being slapped around the salt mines and the laundromat

O Satan, can I have another Snapple please

The locksmith, working on locks, posing before a door you ended up kicking
in, Hoboes in oak trees splicing together a cash register below
The front of Jesus' sure-fire unemployment parade in April

O Satan, one-twenty-five you said? I've got twenty-five

Toiling, the locksmith meets the Mets in the jailyard and in the hearts of girls
Cultivating Monday out of muddy or the love of gunboats on the Nile

O Satan, two slices of plain to go

Jaundiced Grand Marshal whose days in exile are lit up by foreign investors,
Confessor of dusty pensioneers and pope concealors

O Satan, lemme have this size soda

Adopted father of both of them lonelily getting off the bus, which one
carries the cup of black coffee in her suitcase
A craps shooter chased on foot from Duluth to South Dakota?!

O Satan, I need three large pies

Directions

Go down the well-lit corridor and take a right and then up a flight of stairs
　　or two.

If you bump your head on the ceiling, you've gone too far and should turn
　　around. Down near the end of the block

You'll see the entrance to a vacuum store, and to the right the offices of an
　　insurance company.

Take a left at the ATM and past the abandoned building. In the distance
　　you can see an Arby's.

Don't take another step, you're close. At about your nine o'clock there's a
　　store front

And just beyond it a door with a brand new dead bolt. Ring the bell and
　　I'll come down and unlock the door so I can pay you.

La Mort

CXXI
Law Morgue Days Almonds

An orange noose deleted the old blender as it lay in my chair.
Native sons fawned for comely trombones.
Eighty strangled flossers were distracted
By fresh eggs poring out of closets. Suit yourself. Taste your soup bowl.

You saw it, a long week lured into the shower of the new year,
But your notes discourse zero divestment of your flamboyant style.
You rattle like a key in its hole, luring, cheering on laws for dopes looming
        in the mire.
"Damn no dull grasping" says my wash bowl.

Fate arose and ate a plum estate,
News changed hands and a clear moon eeked out,
Commanding its glow over the lawns, over the sand. Too spongy to add,

The apples were tired and the oranges lay around the port. True
Vine dropper, animate and feed all the ages. Why won't you
Let me walk to her knee as an elephant in the mud?

The Death Of The Poor

Over are the bills! And who can make a living these
For an underground newspaper—the burnt out ends
Climbing higher and higher until the batteries
Empty bottles on the soles of our moccasins

In the studio of the hurricane, eating goat
Reason why a vampire licks his plate clean to
Your note book I say the famous surgeon wrote
Barn, eating dormice and their wheatgrass nests, while you

Slippers for a dormouse born with a wooden
In his dreams like eggs crashing down on a wooden
Autumn. The naked and the poor eating away

Temples with a secret added ingredient;
Poor are a uterus that will birth an ancient
A new body that begins at the ankle. Say

The North Of Artists

Fate combines the man who secures sheep bells
And the bailiff lifting his caricature from the bottom. It weighs
As a bee's sting pouring into the end of nature's mysteries.
Combine my quiver and a prober's javelin;

Will an amoeba inform us of the whole rich earth?
We destroy the sea-cow's lurid armature
Before containing the beast. How big,
Not to refill infernal sandlots with our desires.

On the docks the Greek alphabet stares at its idle sons
As chess men demean the face of the theater.
On the docks she styled her breast with a hammer

And at noon she hoped for a strange and somber capitol!
Cast moors off, plunge communism into solitude and rejuvenation.
Charge entrance of blossoms which carve up this air!

CXXIV
The Fin Of The Journey

Under the bell tower's lumpier knee
Courtiers reason the density of sand. Her third
Life cries out. Impudent
Australians, they press their suits into the horizon.

The nut in the voluptuous month
Appeases. All notes indicate the fame
Missing. All notes indicate the hotness.
The Poet twitters: "At last!

My spirit brings this mess of vertebrae,
Invoking ardently its pose in the garden:
The sober, plain songs of funerals.

My vase is better than two Spanish dogs, worse
Than a captain in the bows of his riddles.
O arms and tendons making things new again!"

CXV
Le Rêve D'Un Curieux

À Jen Robinson

What does you know pine tree or conifer melting slowly in de mout'?
And are collection agents repeatedly calling or marking car tires with chalk
      and singing "Oh if only one man wasn't a singing liar!"
I'm on my way to my supermarket my death. Soup, the state was deep in
      enemy territory my love,
And I wanted nothing more than to mix into battle a door a hooker an evil
      doctor in a gully.

Aint it or gosh I here we go and come with me your sole hope we go to
      the beach and I lie to you. I use
More additional all of the milky ways Allah provides us with and leave you
      in sable, knowing I'm a liar
And plus even more tour guides guide the tortugas. A chef in his apron a
      delicatessen, she
All my heart is leaning back into a chair a spider arranges my furniture or
      the world starves off its liars.

I was the state was a small child familiar and fond of the circus.
Had I never breathed in or ridden out or set my hair on fire leaping
      through a burning hoop
Or at least I was swaddled wrapped in newspapers and woke up and arose

I was dead before breakfast. And the sun was late coming up. The wheat
Was all around me. The milk walked on my—Or what?! Wasn't I ever then
      already allowed to curse aloud?
I was out of work, the state, rolling in leaves, and I was at the end of my
      days, again.

CXXVI
Le Voyage

i.

So such the infants immortalized in tan overturned applecart and some stamps
The universe over on the east girl this asia are your vast appetite.
Ah choo! Cue the newsboy. on the east my paint to the tune of Clara
       Barton lighting the lamps!
Old eyes do surrender and cue the newsboy on the tiny eastern seaboard

One morning. My criminal-minded father the cowboy arrived in a casket
       buckling the planks of my porch. The servant boy brought us a
       glass of water stamped out the flames
Drinking hisself silly fat man in a raccoon jacket and then. Stamps out the
       dreams of fishermen
And then a criminal mind packs us all into the Studebaker, swiftly Larry
       has me stamping. My tongue is broke,
Can't kiss this letter. A long train rolls off the boat (I must be in Japan

Lesions, ticklish spots damn-stamping. What does she shave herself one
       country at a time until hungry
Stamping on houses, the horror of their cardboard kisses falling on and
       something more the Huns
As they overestimate the stars the trees ears eyes full in the yearning
       stamping one woman
Singing circles around Herodotus. Daughter and younger daughter
       running circles at least until there are perfumes

For nothing is changed unless you strangle it, beating up the old, sick they
       still deposit money into their bank accounts
In spite of space the stars stamping on and stamping on the light the
       sewers the lighthouse and stamps. Do you see these the embraced?
The ice where they slipped and died, these only the broken dishes Whodat
       these cutting open my rent check envelope.
Slowly I am wiping your lipstick off of my face.

Let's go back to May when the real voyagers aren't songs are soon see ya
       there only who haven't left
From the parking lot. Light hearts, somebody's singing blathering oats
       onto the ballroom,
Stamping but then their end, Parker's been your friend and ever did they
       turn over the cartography? Tea time in the tent
And [why must you keep talking? no one else here is talking and] Saint
       Sebastian why do you always talk and hiss? All aboard!

Seize it all there where the days sire holding the phone out or some undress
And who opens the window again, aint he the one the only one who
        scribbled on the cannon
Stamps vast silver tea services, a check from your aunt money from the
        undressing
And don't fewer prison guards pin his hands to the wall and never to
        the lemons!

ii.

We's imitatin' horror! Singing for my toupee a bowl of soup the lawn
And into their valise and their promises. Same as when in our summertime
Lake Beauregard or the prospect of death tied itself around our necks so
        and the prospect of death rolled
Like an angel. Having cried it all out she unlocked an empty room for us
        the yeti gone crazy

After only one pull at the slots change silver dollars spilling out
        everywhere. Oh but you had to see the place
And, if not stone agey enough neanderthal the cro-magnon held the door
        ajar and maybe even though it doesn't mean a thing to you
Or that man, don't leave the door ajar hope can't be caught with a lariat
        around the foot like a yearling
Or Paul went trout fishing but his letters came back insufficient postage.
        Was I always tipsy when where I curtseyed before we danced. and
        out of my nose a five dollar gold coin

A handbook of knots and easterly a mattress for three but I can't get down
        to the bottom of the Grand Canyon of our love anymore now that
        your mule has gone looking for the mice a wooden clock
One voice already leaping on my eyes on the bridge No music begins
One voice that still retains something of the Hun. Loving and eight ball.
        An Oglala Sioux cries
"In the bog...a battle stuck to my hands...a banner year" Hell. All it is is
        an egg cream school

Checking its pulse at a stop light. The drunks come out of the bars and get
        in their cars, the cops, vigilant
East in an unmarked El Dorado promise to dust them off.
Lemons or Jean Genet or the birth of the dressing room pay-off. The
        envelope, son or giddy
By the treasure trove, I gave birth to a cash register filled with rubies.
        Heading towards morning

Or the pavement again in love, the foots come down around the fireplace
Do we blame him for posting on trees the picture of a wooden-legged man
The bullfight in the parking lot the matador with the soft-pressed swan
      feather boots or the inventor of those damned Vikings?
Doesn't lemon rip up the turf an old house wine disappears a blood-feud
      re-appears or Frère Jacque and we go to the sea?

Tel Aviv the old vagabond putting lint or the Virgin or feet stamp down
      squarely working
Dreams into her nose and ears. The bright air this afternoon on the
      subway there were three not two of them,
Son, or in sorcery the days cover Al Capone's gaze, the belfry,
The stars and fish or the chandelier that illuminates a whorehouse.

iii.
Stunning boy day traders aging seventeen or more! Quieting wheat fields
      devoid of wheat no screaming or crying
We list on shoelaces your yew trees your horse tree pruners up comes the sea!
In Montreal right now. paper cranes. we list your wealth of memories
Those blue eyes shop girls & some school girls those kisses old arounds us
      like the sea Asters bloomed or fallen around us and vapory and
      others. Reason

We take busses we I take you in my mouth stunning young going with no
      smoke trail to swallow I turn around and but there's no more
      there it is you are
Made off, filling the whole crane the between us the in we or no prisons
      the fortresses
Pass out before we hit the pillows legs and arms joints gone to tissue paper
Your recollection you memories go off with the body of the horizon.

Tell me little teeth, what have you got to say for yourself?

iv.
                  "We have seen the new haircuts of the future
And today's floating We've already seen today's fur coat
Eating badly well little chocolates today and stepped into the cheeks the
      cloaks of all velvet and sub-zero architectural cave-ins
We we are softly and often. The wind hoards all young models and
      acquiescent mouths. yes, come hither.

The story of the legs was walking to the bank alone with question. The sea
      was all purple bruises
The story of the legs for days cities tell me point out that when the sun is
      sitting comfortably down
All young models ask into our liquor cabinets or once the garden
      started speaking
Back out of the water coming out the sky the spitting image of a singing
      alley cat.

Money pours into the city, more money, more long passageways longer
      days more lepers cooing
Always never none nothing held back now the Bering straits, others move
      closer along lines of latitude my sterile girl among the masses of
      the masses
For these eyes that see orange hazard signs I soften, disappear with legs
      or laundry.
And the day steps up with lead in his noodle the day draws kisses out from
      our their mouths

—Lagging behind us since a lightning blast adds old gentlemen the police
      force in quatrains.
Dear sir, old trees here in Spain may leap for their own pleasure with
      certain grace
But this depends on the gross profits receipts and how far can you get on
      ten cents, hardly, you're heavy, engorged
Your branches want to see the sun even more than the president.

Angry Grandma steps up with day to the line Grand arbitrator Tree with
      more life than Liberace
Which tree is the president sleeping in? Your aunt pours We have We are
      thirsty at sunset
Cluelessly several chickens flamingos pour into their favourite album of
      Liberace's
Brothers whose trousers and towers find boatswains fallen down at their
      feet all this, wind, the cowardly lion

We have waved good-bye to these days I love or trample
The shortened trombones, constellations cooking up light between us
These northern compadres openly acting their ages openly shouting at a jar
      of olives don't the americans the IRS sing celebratory
Cutting open the straits watering cut flowers while bankers dream of ruin
      Them they

Some costumes that are as the eyes pouring milk on your address
Some women don't lay their teeth and their ogling on elephant tits
And the day shuffles its wise men and Marlene Dietrich with a serpent's caress."

v.

(EF sings JB)

Pwease, Pwease, Pwease, Pwease
  Pwease, Pwease, don' go
Pwease, Pwease, Pwease
  Pwease, Pwease, don' go
Honey Pwease don' go
Yeah, oh yeah, whoa
I wuv you so
  Pwease, Pwease, don' go

Baby you did me wong
  You know you done me wong
Whoa, whoa, you done me wong
  You know you done me wong
You know you done, done me wong
Whoa, whoa, oh yeah
Took my wuv and now you'we gone
  Pwease, Pwease, don' go

Pwease, Pwease, Pwease, Pwease, Pwease
  Pwease, Pwease, don' go
Pwease, Pwease, Pwease, Pwease, Pwease
  Pwease, Pwease, don' go
Honey Pwease don' go
Whoa, oh yeah, Wowd
I wuv you so
  Pwease, Pwease, don' go

I just wanna heah you say aye
  Pwease, Pwease, don' go
Aye, aye, aye, aye, aye, aye, aye, aye
  Pwease, Pwease, don' go
Honey Pwease don' go
Oh, oh, yeah
I wuv you so
  Pwease, Pwease, don' go

Baby take my hand
  Pwease, Pwease, don' go
I wanna be your wuving man, oh yeah
  Pwease, Pwease, don' go
Dawwing Pwease don' go
Oh, yeah, oh

I wuv you so
>> *Pwease, Pwease, don' go*

Pwease ... don' go
>> *Pwease, Pwease, don' go*
Pwease ... don' go
>> *Pwease, Pwease, don' go*
Honey Pwease don' go
I wuv you so
>> *Pwease, Pwease, don' go*
Pwease, Pwease

vi.
>> "Out of the cervix out of the soda fountain

A pour not open or working The main thing the money
We've got to see especially, a parakeet a pelican, and without this or having
>> looked in the church key for them
We're heading North, up to the ocean's surface in the bathtub The farmer
>> tints his wife's story with an eggshell white.
At least look clearly at the knees of your enemies, at theirs, at the farmer
>> his deathly salesmanship

His wife locked up in a sea cave where the cleaning lady an orangutang
>> an organ player with sleeves rolled up and in the know. The know
>> or swimming
But not laughing or sad or smelling bad and don't they love you and won't
>> they go hungry for you
Long before you try and sing for your supper, drowning, a pail. I can wait
>> for your urine sample
In an underwater cave in an underwater cave. in the bath and Russians
>> swing in to steal my waffle.

Working in the hen house a lock filled with sweet wine, or lemons Listen
>> I'll smash your locks if you don't give me that bloody telegram
Lafayette! What assassin ringing a doorbell and smoking or driving leaves
>> me this note
The fish heading North under its own power disquieted the President in
>> his socks
And leapt up to have more of us rinse our champagne out of the sink

Mostly realigning the wagging tongues on our left

Or everyone climbing the stairs slowly or glockenspiels or the last saint of
 the spring
Pauses in an unlit room with a feather. Under the train, the cat or I sever
 the light
In the unfinished clouds and the crime of it is her pettiforgeries looking to
 fill up a tea cosy

Or hanging above us. The Bavarians I've referred to or having come down
 from a vaporous heritage
And, fell through the floor in disrepair, my ceiling aint it like she was out
 of her jurisdiction
Screaming, donchaknow or sneezing and in comes the game warden again,
 under water, his hues:
'O mine and some say nothing endlessly, o mine Montmartre, I the
 bathwater could be warmer'

And at least bath salts, or a decent mountain a day a seance that means
 something
In the Furies' root cellar Foghorn Leghorn runs aground tripping on his
 rain hat or parks the Dodge by the dustbin
And hides out the immense puddle down his thigh is immense!
—The telephone is due East lit up in stages from within or the tern or a
 tin egg in a coin slot."

vii.
Having seen her on the cell phone the Southern the blue silver Can she
 change a tire so we might get moving?!
She can lean on me or call me alone and at a baseball game the pitcher
 only yesterday I pushed open the door an oil baron
Yesterday, hers, tomorrow, or at the end of the day with shoes off We're
 making out! Look! Write down what you imagine
To be where the water is The murderer is The dancing a desert our lunch
 hour aflame beside him

And why was he must he take off now? Won't stay? If you're too poor to
 stay, stay
Padre, open the window and climb down if need be the courtyard
 surrounds the building, and the author washes up and drinks a
 long draught from the fountain
Washing the soles of his boots and walks wet tracking into the house I owe
 you twenty dollars for looking around all night and night at the
 Kabuki theater
Off to work! At least Mount St. Helens is decorating is without dinner again

Like the young juniper tree lost wandered off into the dollar store where
       the apostles
And no one knew them, put them all into a suitcase, kicked the tires on a
       station wagon kicked a hole in a boat
And only all fruits the friar ate or he retained too much water or the
       refrigerator caught flames creeping up the dusted back It makes no
       sense to reel in the others,
Who knows if the plumb bob left the office with any of them a kiss

Then until he puts his foot through the monitor.
Is the lynch mob going to pour another bowl of cereal for the Railroad
       Baron? Is Spain Are acres spreading before us
Is the hydrofoil equipped with a quadruple-redundant or the same before
       we pour a bowl for the Great Wall? of China?
Leslie's eyes are fixing fix the hole in the orange the eating the horseman
       and then open up the wind

The lynch mob doubles and encircles or strays an old hound Surely you
       meant me or my arms, my stars? Braying
With the courtesans joining in too loud a young passenger, she
Do you hear yourself? This voice, charming or and I remember it
       entertaining baying
Who was singing: "For ice cream! Do you want to eat it

In an empty lot? us and all of us stand smoking! Is it ice cream that keeps
       you on the verge of being a flower
The miracle, fruits Don't you ever write your dog's name at the end of
       letters to your family?
When you part the curtains the room lights up A lawnmower or grass the
       deuce the eight the cards spread out over the prairies
This afternoon seventeen afternoons The lock the key wake me when it's
       time to go to bed."

All currencies all monetary units are well known the lynch mob looks for
       water the well A ghost
We plow the stars, ours, over there lying on its back stroking your arms
       holding you down by your wrists Towards us
"Another lemonade and your dog is swimming in the tub with the
       toaster oven"
Then cellmates talking doesn't the jade or the lynch mob bathes the sons
       of the philanthropist.

viii.

O Mort, old and vying captain, it's time, lift up the anchor!
This country is irritating Mort! Let's dress one another in our mother's curtains!
If the sky tries to sell us or eat the sea aren't we night or black like a crusty
Northern Sea dog you met on the gangway stuffing his pockets with
      silk flowers?

Each line knots itself around my neck your fish write mercury in my brain
      Piano forte
Hangs me from its clotheslines we want, my dead aunt and I a few fires to
      broil the cervix
To drown in the fountain drunk Heaven or Hell, who gives a fuck?
We're fond of not knowing and keep digging in our empty pockets for the
      desert or the flood.

AFTERWORD

I. Early Methods

In April of 1990, I received a postcard from Jackson Mac Low. He and I had been writing back and forth intermittently following his having taught at the university I was attending. In his note, Jackson asked if I had copies of his *French Sonnets* or *Words nd Ends from Ez*, and if not, would I like him to send them to me? I didn't have either of the books and soon wrote back to say that I'd love to have them.

It wasn't long after replying to his postcard that I began wondering about the books now headed my way. In the past I'd noticed that the titles of Jackson's books or sequences often bore some relation not only to the content of the poems, but also to the methods he'd employed in writing them.[1] I already knew something about *Words nd Ends from Ez*, having heard Jackson speak of these poems and having read the ones included in *Representative Works: 1938-1985*, but I'd never heard of *French Sonnets*, so I became especially curious about the book. What about the poems would be French? In what ways would they be sonnets? I looked in local book stores and in the university's library but couldn't find a copy of the book. While I was waiting for the books to show up in the mail I kept thinking about the poems, and I began to imagine several methods Jackson might have used in writing them. Later on that same month I decided I would put one of these imagined methods to use myself.

Several years earlier I'd stolen my mother's copy of Charles Baudelaire's *Les Fleurs du Mal*, an all-French edition[2] put out by Doubleday in 1961. Opening the book I chose a poem at random: "Le Serpent Qui Danse." Starting with the poem's title, I went through *The Random House Collegiate Dictionary* looking for each of the words in the poem. Obviously, since I was using an English dictionary, I wasn't able to find most of them. Instead I located the word that would have followed Baudelaire's alphabetically, had it been in the dictionary. Once I'd located this English word I wrote it into my translation in the same location its French partner had occupied in the original. In this way in the title "Serpent" was replaced with "Serpent," and "Danse" was replaced with "Dap." I didn't change proper nouns. When I located an English word for use and saw that it was noted in the dictionary as having French origins and that its spelling hadn't changed when it crossed over to English, I substituted the word that followed it alphabetically in the dictionary.[3] I began all this quite late at night and discovered that the method was rather time-consuming, so I went to bed with only the first two stanzas of the poem completed.

MWord

The next morning a second, faster method occurred to me. I realized that, rather than looking up each word in a dictionary, I could type one of Baudelaire's poems—in French—into a word-processing program and using the "spell-check" feature allow the program to make English "suggestions" for each of the "misspelled" words. I could then choose to replace the French words with those suggested by the word processor.

I selected Baudelaire's "L'Aube Spirituelle" at random and typed it up using *Microsoft Word v.3.0*. I soon discovered, however, that when the program spell-checked the poem there were some French words for which the program wouldn't offer an English suggestion. I went through the entire poem taking *Word*'s suggested substitutions whenever they were offered, but ended up with a series of lines written in both French and English. I translated the remaining French words directly into English using *Larousse's French-English/English-French Dictionary*. The resulting lines were made up entirely of English words, but they lacked coherent syntax. At this point, in spite of my interest in using methods similar to this one as a way of getting away from the practices I'd employed as a poet up to that point, I didn't feel completely satisfied with the result. My interest in having a strong hand in the poem and in narrative kept me from being content with the text as it stood.

Later I came to think of this text—seemingly unconnected English words—as my "base text." I used this "base text" as a sort of framework for the resultant poem. This isn't to say that I would use each word from each line of the base text in strict order, but rather that I allowed the words to suggest lines of the poem to me, although individual words from the base text were sometimes directly incorporated. In this way the word "mess" in line 11 of "L'Aube Spiritually" comes from spell-checking the French "mes," whereas my use of "electrifying" was suggested by "voltage," the spell-checker's substitution for the French "voltige" in the original.

Much later, after I'd used this method a few times, I stopped using the French-English dictionary to translate words remaining in French after the spell-check was complete. Instead, I started translating these French words in a way which more closely resembled the **As Understood** and **Free** translation methods described below. After I'd written my first twenty translations I stopped using the **MWord** method much, though I did return to it from time to time when I needed to briefly change my practice.

Phonetic

For whatever reason, after writing "L'Aube Spiritually" I didn't write another of these translations until late October of the same year. When I did decide to pick things up again I was nowhere near a computer. Since I couldn't generate a base text using the familiar spell-check method, I chose to do so by trying to find English phonetic equivalents of Baudelaire's French. Sounding out the words to "La Mort Des Amants" (which I'd again selected at random, of course[4]) I generated a base text of English words which, again, lacked any obvious syntax. I listened for English words in the sounds of individual words, strings of words, or any sequence of syllables in the words in Baudelaire's lines. In this manner the beginning of the first line of "La Mort Des Amants," "Nous aurons des lits..." was translated as "Noose orange delete." Using these words as a jumping-off point, "An orange noose deleted..." became the beginning of the first line of "Law Morgue Days Almonds."

As Understood

The next method that I came up with was far simpler than the previous two. I should back up a bit and say that when I began this project it had been about three years since my last French class. While my pronunciation might have been acceptable, there were large holes in my comprehension of French.[5] In looking over several of Baudelaire's poems however, I realized that I still understood a passable amount of what I was reading, and those words or phrases that I didn't recognize were automatically assigned meanings, which they may or may not have had.[6] Not unlike a poorly prepared student translating a passage he's never seen before from French to English in an exam, I tried to make sense of the poems in front of me. Since I was trying to translate the phrases in their entirety, I didn't need a base text to work from. At this point I was more interested in understanding the language in Baudelaire's poems than just the individual, isolated words.

Word List

The fourth method I worked out was only used in two of my translations: "Ember" and "Checkroom." I made three lists of words (one list each for nouns, verbs and adjectives) chosen at random from *The Random House Collegiate Dictionary*. Each list had twenty-six words that began with a different letter of the alphabet, making a table three columns wide and twenty-six rows long. Taking Baudelaire's poems "Elevation" and "Causerie," I replaced the French nouns, verbs and adjectives with nouns, verbs and adjectives from my word lists. I chose words that began with the letter corresponding with the 1st letter of each French word. So "Elevation" became "Ember," because "Elevation" was a noun beginning with E, and "Ember" was the word in the noun column's E row. Adverbs were mostly translated as adjectives; prepositions and conjunctions were translated literally; and articles were translated as I judged appropriate, because "la vie" could translate as "life" or "the life" in different contexts. While my adherence to use of punctuation had varied in methods employed prior to "Word List," the punctuation in both "Ember" and "Checkroom" mimics that of Baudelaire's originals, and there's probably also a close adherence to the sentence structures of the originals, due to the very nature of such a one-to-one replacement.

Free[7]

If it's not already evident—after my confessing that I decided to use a word processor to find my French words' nearest neighbors rather than search for the space they would each occupy in a dictionary—let me say straight out that I can become somewhat impatient as a writer.[8] I found that as I translated poems **As Understood** or used the base texts generated with **MWord** or the **Phonetic** method, I wanted to move a little more quickly through the poems. New words and lines were suggesting themselves to me based on the meanings, sounds, shapes, possible meanings, and associations with the language in the French originals. So the **Free** method was developed by allowing myself to make use of these "suggestions" in what I came to think of as a "rapid jumping-off from the text." While the translations I had made **As Understood** were written based on my best understanding of the poems, the **Free** translations responded more to characteristics of Baudelaire's writing which were less obvious or overt. For example, the title of the poem "The Auto Mechanics," translated **Free** from "L'Héautontimorouménos," may have arrived as a result of the presence of "auto" in the longer French word, the length of the word and the other letters in Baudelaire's title word, or perhaps something I am unaware of, to which I was responding.

Since there is no grounding rule in the **Free** method, in the later translation work there was plenty of room to modify, respond or react both to modes of writing that I'd employed previously in the project and my experience of translating the poems. **Free** is the method used predominantly in *Flowers of Bad*, and there is no definitive version of it. Variations include **Frigid**, **Frigidaire**, **Frozen**, and **Cracked**. One poem was even translated using the **Shazbot** translation method. On the pages where I first wrote out my **Free** translations there are often notes like "What has Free become?" or "Free, but slowly," or once or twice something like "Free-slurry." There are probably numerous changes in my use of the **Free** method that could be noted if these translations were regarded chronologically, including breakdowns in syntax and in the one-to-one translation of words or images.

Sometimes two or more meanings suggested themselves for lines or phrases in a poem, and rather than trying to figure out which of them was *le mot juste*, I would incorporate more than one, covering all my bets.

While it's true that many of the methods that came later were developed as direct responses to ones that had preceded them, I think of the creation of the of the first six methods (the discarded first one with the dictionary, **MWord, Phonetic, Word List, As Understood, Free**) as evolving more than responding. I say this because the development of each came more out of working with the previous methods and seeing other routes or possibilities than out of reacting against them in frustration or trying to find some way to get around problems that I'd come up against. The **Free** method grew mostly out of translating Baudelaire's poems **As Understood**, although the other five methods contributed something to my use of it I'm sure.

II. Later Methods

Collision & Directed

It has always seemed impossible to me to translate something without imposing some part of the translator's own disposition. With this in mind, I decided that I wanted to intentionally choose a direction or attitude for a translation to adopt before I began composing it. The Collision method involved taking a poem of Baudelaire's along with a second text, and translating the first either by using the second as a filter, or by smashing the two together during the translation.

Somewhat similarly, the **Directed** method became another way of imposing a leaning or a tendency on a translation. In a **Directed** translation everything is interpreted in terms of a particular focus. If this focus were, for example, the object of one's affection or a particular political agenda then it would be as if it were *known* that Baudelaire's poem was in fact about the object of one's affection or the political agenda. Any further understanding of Baudelaire's poem would reflect this fact and this premise would be demonstrated in the translation of Baudelaire's poem.

Blind

At some point I decided that I'd translated enough of Baudelaire's poems that I felt as though I knew what he was doing, and I felt as though I understood pretty much what I was doing, so why not simply cut out the middle man? For the **Blind** translations I approached Baudelaire's poem knowing nothing more at first than the line count and the title. Once I had written my translation I checked it against Baudelaire's original and any parts of the poem that had been translated incorrectly were then corrected. (Remarkably, the handful of times that I used this method I found that my translations were pretty much dead-on and required very little correction.)

Forced Sonnet

In order to explain the **Forced Sonnet**[9] method, it may be easiest to first describe the form of the resulting poem. The **Forced Sonnets** were translated from sonnets of Baudelaire's. The translations all had 14 lines, followed the same rhyme scheme and each line of the translation had the same number of syllables as the corresponding line in the French poem.

I would begin by taking a translation I had done of one of Baudelaire's sonnets using any of the other methods I've described up to this point (let's call this the *old translation*). Then from the beginning of the first line of my old translation, I counted out a number of syllables equal to the number of syllables in the first line of the original French poem, and struck out all words on the line that came after. The words that remained became the first line of the **Forced Sonnet**. I then followed the same procedure with the second line of my old translation as I had with the first to produce the second line of my **Forced Sonnet**.

Starting at the beginning of the third line of the old translation, I would look for a word which rhymed with what was now the last word of the first line of the **Forced Sonnet**. I then counted backwards from the rhyming word on the third line until I had reached a syllable count equal to the number of syllables in the third line of Baudelaire's original. Only the syllables within that count made up the third line of the **Forced Sonnet** and I would strike out all others from the line. I then followed the same procedure to produce the fourth line as I had with the third, beginning by seeking a word in fourth line of the old translation which rhymed with the last word of the second line of the **Forced Sonnet**.

Following this procedure I would now have a four-line stanza of two rhyming couplets, A-B-A-B. From here I would go on to produce the remaining rhyming couplets of the **Forced Sonnet** (i.e., C-D-C-D E-E-F G-G-F). This is the basic method. However, there were a few contingencies I discovered I needed to plan for.

Let's suppose that I found a word in the third line of the old translation which rhymed with the end word of the new first line of the **Forced Sonnet**. Now let's suppose that counting backwards from that word in the old translation I arrived at the beginning of the line before I have matched the syllable count of the corresponding third line of Baudelaire's poem. In this instance I would wrap my syllable count around to the end of the line, continuing to count backwards from the last word of the third line of the old translation. The last syllable in that count would become the beginning of the third line in the **Forced Sonnet** and the rhyming word—where we started our count—would become the end of the third line.

As an example, let's say my first line of my **Forced Sonnet** ended with the word "these" and the third line of my old translation is "The batteries on the furnace climbing higher and higher until." The first word in this line that rhymes with "these" is "batteries." But if the third line in Baudelaire's poem has thirteen syllables I'm out of luck, because counting backwards from "batteries" is only going to give me four syllables: "The batteries." So I'll get my remaining nine syllables by continuing to count backwards from "until," the last word of the same line in the old translation. Counting backwards nine syllables I get "Climbing higher and higher until." I'll strike all remaining words or syllables from the line and put these nine syllables before my first four (still gotta have "batteries" at the end of the line to make the rhyme) and get as the third line of my **Forced Sonnet**:

Climbing higher and higher until the batteries

Now let's suppose that there is no word in the third line of my old translation which rhymes with the end word of the first line of the **Forced Sonnet** I'm composing. In this case I would return to the first line of my old translation and re-write it by starting the syllable count from the second word in the line. This should produce a different end-word for the first line of the **Forced Sonnet**. So then I would return to the third line of the old translation and try to find a rhyming match again. If again no rhyming match could be found, I would return to the first line of the old translation and begin my count with the third word, repeating the process until a match had been made.

Finally, it may have occurred to the reader that the odds are good that the syllable count might at some point fall in the middle of a word. I approached this issue both possible ways, by composing **Forced Sonnets** that included portions of words and by extending the syllable count in order to accommodate entire words. However, I never used both approaches in any one **Forced Sonnet**.

The Two Good Sisters

The Two Good Sisters method gets its name from both the title of the poem this method was first used with ("Les Deux Bonnes Sœurs") and because the lines of a poem translated this way are separated in the middle by a short gap, creating a poem that may look as though it's made up of two distinct but related parts, one right next to the other.

In employing **The Two Good Sisters**, I would take a rectangular and opaque object (i.e., a magazine or a book) and lay it over a poem of Baudelaire's so that the object's leftmost edge ran vertically down the center of the poem, covering up the right half of the poem from top to bottom. I then translated (using any of my other methods) only what remained uncovered, including those words that were only partially visible. Once the entire first half of every line in the poem had been translated this way, I covered only the left half of the poem and translated the right-hand part of the poem which was now visible.

From there, I lined the two halves of the poem up alongside one another with a gap of about five em spaces. With one or two of the translations I composed using **The Two Good Sisters** I merged the two halves together by removing the gap so they had the appearance of being made up of unbroken lines. In other instances I attempted to resolve the two mismatched halves of the lines so that they seemed to make more sense narratively; in others I didn't, allowing them to make their own sense.

Another variation of this form worth mentioning is **The One Blind Sister**, where one half of the poem was translated using **The Two Good Sisters** method and the other was translated using the **Blind** method (as explained above).

Exclusion

Somewhat similar in appearance, but not to be mistaken for **The Two Good Sisters** is the **Exclusion** method. The two might easily be mistaken because of a similarity in their appearances: both may include a visible split in the poem's lines.

The **Exclusion** method was accomplished in two stages. In the first stage of the translation process, I allowed myself not to feel bound to making use of all aspects of Baudelaire's original poem. I took instead whichever parts of the lines I wanted and disregarded the rest. I tried, however, to insure that the result of this first stage would be a poem which would cohere narratively as the reader read in normal fashion, left to right, top to bottom. In the second stage of the **Exclusion** method I returned to the beginning of Baudelaire's poem and wrote separate translations of the portions of the lines I'd excluded in the first stage, without trying to force the translated portions to reflect or cohere with any other part of the poem. Once the excluded portions had all been translated, I placed them next to the corresponding lines of the first part of the translation in italics, enclosed within parentheses.

Swimming

This may be the most difficult of the methods to describe exactly or specifically. I called the method **Swimming** because this is how I thought of it at the time: as swimming on the surface of the poem. Generally I would write out in French one of Baudelaire's poems by hand, in blocks of about four to six lines. Then, using a different color ink, above or below the copied lines, I would write lines which somehow captured the mood of the French, while paying as little direct attention as I could to those qualities of the language that I had paid attention to in earlier methods (meanings, sounds, shapes, etc.). I repeated this process until all the lines from Baudelaire's poem had been written out in French and translated in order.

Anagrammatic

I had intended for the **Anagrammatic** translations to be the last method I employed. By the time I reached the point where there were only five untranslated poems I had developed many feelings about the practice and process of translating, and about what I had and had not been able to accomplish during the long project of working with *Les Fleurs Du Mal.* I regretted that in my translations so many things had been added and so many things lost. I wanted somehow to make use of all of a poem without losing or adding anything.

The closest that I came to this ideal may be in the **Anagrammatic** translations (there are 4), as every letter that appears in the original French poem also appears in the translation. No letters were added. These translations have titles which are anagrams of the French originals' and every poem is a line-by-line anagram of its French counterpart. I didn't retain any of the accents or cedillas, and letters such as œ were converted into o and e, but with these exceptions each line in the translation contains the same letters as the original.

The first poem I translated using the **Anagrammatic** method used a variant that clearly follows the toughest set of restrictions, bordering on the Oulipian.[10] In "A.M. Sequel," not only is every line, dedication and epigram anagrammatic of the original, but the poem is made up of complete sentences which follow the rules of English grammar (although there continues to be some debate between my copy-editor mother and myself as to whether a single noun can be modified by two verbs without a conjunction). All of the **Anagrammatic** translations were written by laying out letters from the lines of one of Baudelaire's poems using the tiles from two complete *Scrabble*™ sets and then re-arranging them. I did this steadily for about three and a half months in order to write "A.M. Sequel," and then swore I would never take up this particular variation of the method again.

As I've just written, when I began the **Anagrammatic** poems I had many complex feelings about translating and more specifically about translating Baudelaire. I also felt that composing false translations had often been a way of finding entry into a poem from which I was otherwise excluded. From time to time, however, I no longer wanted so much to find a way into the poems as to shatter them with a hammer. Though I tried to figure out just how this could be accomplished ("1. Write poem out on a sheet of glass. 2. Apply hammer as needed.", etc.) I never fully succeeded. I do think, however, that the remaining three **Anagrammatic** translations ("Hep Slears," "XLII" & "Er Irbralaple") come closest to accomplishing this out of all the translations that I've done.[11]

Re-translation

There at the last though, I found that there were a few poems that I wanted to re-translate, although I found the methods that I'd used up to that point unworkable, perhaps because I was quite ready to be finished with the project. I tried working with the texts as they were, colliding them with alternate translations of the same poem, extracting words, etc. The results, however, were not terribly satisfying. Ultimately I ended up re-translating them, but without referring again to Baudelaire's original. Two of these (there were three, I believe) were translated from English into English, using a method which probably owes something to the **Swimming** method. The third of these **Re-translations** I translated back into French. Having read all of Baudelaire's *Les Fleurs du Mal* in one fashion or another, I had picked up or remembered a bit more French than I started with. If nothing else I might say that I felt a certain familiarity with the language, even if I wouldn't be able to share that familiarity with anyone else by engaging them in a conversation.[12] I decided that I would do my best to restore one of Baudelaire's poems by re-translating it from English back into French in a way which may serve as the obverse of the **As Understood** method.

III. A Final Note On The Forms Of These Poems

With few exceptions I have managed from the beginning to retain several aspects of Baudelaire's form in each of these poems. Firstly, almost every line in this collection begins with an initial cap, as do the lines in the edition of *Les Fleurs du Mal* that I have used throughout the process. For the most part I have also followed Baudelaire's line breaks and stanza length. His sonnets remain sonnets here, at least in as much as they are fourteen-line poems in two four-line stanzas followed by two three-line stanzas.[13] While all these poems were translated as whole and complete poems, the translations were done line by line, and the translated aspects or words from one line do not wrap around and appear on another that follows it. There are also those poems that retain the rhyme schemes of the originals, including some that are not **Forced Sonnets**.

In March of 1991, almost two weeks after I'd written "The Fin of the Journey," the last poem in the first sequence of twenty poems from this series which would later be published as *Flurries of Mail*, a copy of *French Sonnets* that Jackson had sent arrived in the mail.

David Cameron
Toronto, Ontario
December 22, 2001

Footnotes

[1] The title of *Words nd Ends from Ez*, for example, mimics something of the appearance of the lines of the poems included in that collection where Jackson "systematically brought into *Words nd Ends from Ez* letter strings consisting of single words and/or ends of words [from *The Cantos*] that successively 'spell out' Ezra Pound's first and last name 'diastically,' i.e., strings in which the letters of Pound's first and last names occupy places corresponding to those they fill in the names." [*Words nd Ends from Ez*, p. 89]

[2] The only other all-French book of poems that I had in my apartment at the time was Jacques Prevert's *Paroles*. I imagine that this would now be a very different collection if I'd chosen to make use of it rather than *Les Fleurs du Mal*. You might very well be holding a book right now entitled Parolees or Pay Roll instead.

[3] Which leaves us with the mystery of Serpent, which would seem to be a French word which hasn't changed its spelling. Sixteen years later I seem to have lost track of my copy of *The Random House Collegiate Dictionary*, so I'm unable to refer back to exactly what it said. However, other dictionaries that I have in my possession at present indicate that "serpent" is Middle English in origin, and this may be why I chose to keep it in. Or maybe I ignored my rule or hadn't come up with it before I started out writing the translation but found a need to apply it later on so developed it on-the-fly. Christ, it was only eight lines I got through that night. In any event I was probably quite tired and should be cut a small measure of slack for that reason if no other.

[4] Of course, choosing a poem "at random" usually meant opening the book somewhere near the middle and using whichever poem was on the right hand page, so long as it wasn't too lengthy for however much time I wanted to spend writing right then.

[5] Maybe it would be good to include some note about how much French I speak now or had studied up to that point. I had taken about three years of French in high school, and was pretty fanatical about it. I loved studying French, and did very well with it. When I got to college I continued my studies, beginning with a French intensive class and then two more classes over the next two terms, the last one being a class in French phonetics and pronunciation. I left the university I was attending after that third term, largely because the academic mood was somewhat lacking there and my performance academically had begun to slip at the end of my first year. I didn't fail anything, but my studies of French weren't really proceeding with the same vigor that they had when I was in high school. After I got to Binghamton, where I later studied with Jackson, I really didn't feel much like continuing with my French studies. Just before I met Jackson, I had taken a term and a half of introductory Spanish, taken largely because I wanted to be able to better hear the language in Federico Garcia Lorca's poems. As much as I may have wanted to return to my studies of French once I'd begun this project, I felt as though I shouldn't try to learn any more French as it would make the process of translating, especially with the **As Understood** and **Free** methods, that much more difficult. I have only ever read one paragraph of a quotation of Baudelaire's in translation. I have a good understanding of French grammar and at least a fair understanding of the phonetics (although I might not be able to get my tongue to work out all pronunciations as I would like it to). What is probably most lacking is my vocabulary. A somewhat more concrete example of how lacking or not my French is might be found in the poem "Blanche."

⁶In explaining this process to people since, I've pointed out that this is the sort of thing that goes on all the time. I think that when people encounter language they don't understand they automatically make some sense of it, even if they write these interpretations off because they don't match the rest of their understanding.

⁷How shall I explain the Free method now as I hurtle towards Toronto in a train to visit my grandmother just before Christmas? Canada's a strange place, where most of the product packaging (if not all, I haven't inspected it all yet) is written out in both French and English. My earliest desires to study French arose out of a frustration with this country, where left to my own devices while the adults busied themselves with adult matters (all that talking!) I was allowed to sit down in my grandmother's study and watch television. Is there some sort of metaphor for the Free process or for all of false translation in the fact that across North America it seems that the major television stations broadcast much of the same programming but at different times and on differently numbered channels? My grandmother's house possessed a strange device known as a cable box. I don't think that I've ever seen one outside of Canada like it. It was a small box, covered with buttons, each designated with a number and a few letters, probably including ABC, NBC and PBS, but all with the numbers wrong. Since all the stations were wrong, were not where they should have been, I had to punch through this series of buttons trying to uncover the code that would show me the sort of programming I most desired: cartoons. Because of the fervor with which I searched, I don't think that it took too very long to locate a channel showing cartoons, but my discovery was accompanied by a powerful frustration. The cartoons were entirely in French. Bugs and Elmer were speaking, but the words that came out of their mouths were entirely incomprehensible to me. At that point I became determined to learn to speak French, so I could return to Toronto and understand the French cartoons.

So it would be possible, I suppose, to argue that the origin of these false translations comes earlier than when I received Jackson's post card. Fairly late into the project I began to see one possible way of interpreting this project as a struggle to find a way into a text from which I was otherwise excluded. Often enough, this is why I had to switch up or modify my methods, or develop new ones. After working with a method for a while I would find myself stalling out, I would worry that I was falling back on tricks or ways that I already knew would work, and the poems would no longer surprise me in the way that I wanted them to. I am reminded here, oddly enough, of the *Star Trek* villains The Borg, who could be hit by the Enterprise's phaser blasts, but only for a couple of shots, at which point their shields adapted, and the phasers would no longer be useful. So the crew of the Enterprise found that they had to continually change the modulation of their phasers so that they would be able to fight off the Borg and resist being assimilated into their "collective," an organization that thought with one mind, acted as one entity, had only one understanding. Although I wonder if this contradicts a statement by Walt Whitman that I've often also associated with these poems "The job of the poet to resolve all tongues into his own." Though that's "resolve," and not "assimilate."

⁸Although the three and a half months it took to write the **Anagrammatic** "A.M. Sequel" might seem to contradict that.

⁹This description assumes an A-B-A-B first stanza. It should be modified for other Sonnet forms.

¹⁰It's ridiculous to assume that I'm going to be able to explain to you in full what

the Oulipo is or what I mean by Oulipian here, so let's abandon that as the goal of this footnote. Rather I'll refer you to a few other people's words on the subject. In *The Oulipo and Combinatorial Art* (1991) Jacques Roubaud explains that the Oulipo is a group whose name derives from their "initial, inaugural name: Ouvroir de Littérature Potentielle" (Workshop for Potential Literature). He further goes on to explain that "The aim of Oulipo is to invent (or reinvent) restrictions of a formal nature and propose them to enthusiasts interested in composing literature." Raymond Queneau's definition is my favorite: "Oulipians: rats who build the labyrinth form which they plan to escape." In short, when I say "borders on the Oulipian" I mean that the form I was using had several rigid constraints which affected the resulting poem. In truth my constraints were more restrictive I believe than many of the methods created by the Oulipians, though certainly not as restrictive as some. *La Disparition* is a 300 page novel, written in 1969 by Georges Perec, entirely without the letter e. Its translation into English by Gilbert Adair, also entirely without the letter e, is entitled *A Void*.

I first encountered the Oulipo around 1999, when Harry Mathews came to read at the St. Marks Poetry Project in New York shortly after the publication of *Oulipo Compendium*. I later wrote Mr. Mathews trying to learn whether my anagramatic method had already been developed by any members of the Oulipo. He assured me that it had not.

[11] Ironically this is done without losing any of the "shards" or "fragments" of the original.

[12] I have been asked to include the following tale as an example of how well I actually speak French:

Some years ago, on my first visit to France I went to Avignon in the South. While walking across a bridge that spanned the Rhône and a small park on one bank I was distracted by a group of older men and women playing boules on the grass below. With my head turned to the side and not watching where I was going I walked straight into a lamppost and banged my head so hard that it made a loud "bong!" sound against the metal pole, not unlike the sound of a medium-sized bell being struck. When I recovered from the collision I could see that all the people down in the park below me had paused in their game and were now looking straight up at me, trying to determine what had caused the noise.

Of course I knew that I was going to get a large bump on my head and thought that as self-conscious as I was being an American travelling alone in France, being an American travelling alone in France with a large egg-shaped protrusion on one side of his head would be far worse. I determined immediately that I needed to remedy the situation and set out in search of a bar.

It was late afternoon and fortunately there was one open just past the end of the bridge. I walked in and got the attention of the bartender and he came over, staring fixedly at my growing lump. Now that I had his attention I asked him (in French) "Can I have some ice cream? I've just kicked myself in the head with a lamppost."

[13] There are a couple of exceptions to this "sonnet rule" which were translated in reverse, from the bottom up, so the line order in those stanzas runs three-three-four-four, or where the line order within each stanza remains the same but where the order of the stanzas is reversed.

Photo: Holly White

A native of Brooklyn, David Cameron continues to work and live there with his wife Holly. In 2005 he was the recipient of a Fellowship in Poetry from the New York Foundation for the Arts. He is also the author of the shorter collections *L.P.* and *Several Ghouls Hardly Worth Mentioning*. This is his first full-length collection of poems.